MIRACLE STORIES FROM THE BIBLE

5

Additional materials have been prepared by:
Bob Coffen (Word Searches)
Sally Dillon (puzzles)
Gerald Wheeler (A Closer Look).

Special biblical and archaeological consultants:
Douglas Clark
Larry Herr
Siegfried Horn
Sakae Kubo
Pedrito Maynard-Reid
Ronald Springett
Warren Trenchard
Douglas Waterhouse

Bible stories by Ruth Redding Brand
Professor Appleby narrative by Charles Mills

Professor Appleby and Maggie B Series

1. *Mysterious Stories From the Bible*
2. *Amazing Stories From the Bible*
3. *Love Stories From the Bible*
4. *Adventure Stories From the Bible*
5. *Miracle Stories From the Bible*

MIRACLE STORIES
FROM THE BIBLE

RUTH REDDING BRAND
CHARLES MILLS

REVIEW AND HERALD® PUBLISHING ASSOCIATION
HAGERSTOWN, MD 21740

The author assumes full responsibility for the accuracy of all facts
and quotations as cited in this book.

Names have been supplied characters in some of the Bible stories.
While the names reflect those used during the story's particular time period, the author is not suggesting that anyone in the story was actually
so named.

This book was
Edited by Gerald Wheeler
Designed by Patricia S. Wegh
Cover design by Ron J. Pride
Cover illustration by Kim Justinen
Inside illustrations by Joe Van Severen
Typeset:11/13 Stone Informal

PRINTED IN U.S.A.

01 00 99 98 97   10 9 8 7 6 5 4 3 2 1

Library of Congress Cataloging in Publication Data
Brand, Ruth Redding, 1941-
     Miracle stories from the Bible/Ruth Redding Brand and Charles Mills.
         p. cm.—(Professor Appleby and Maggie B series; 5)
     Summary: Friends gather to hear tape recordings of Maggie B telling various
Bible stories, including those of Moses, Jezebel, and Elisha.

     1. Bible stories, English. 2. Miracles—Juvenile literature. [1. Bible stories.]
I. Mills, Charles, 1950-   . II. Title. III. Series: Brand, Ruth Redding, 1941-   Professor
Appleby and the Maggie B tapes; 5.
     BS551.2.B726 1997
     220.9' 505—dc21   96-52247
                                                                                  CIP
                                                                                   AC

ISBN 0-8280-0961-9

① Basket Case

What's in the basket?" Stacey asked, eyeing the long wicker container held tightly in her grandfather's hands. "Are we going on a picnic?"

The old man shook his head from side to side, then lifted a finger to his lips. "No," he whispered, "we're not going on a picnic."

Stacey's two classmates and best friends, Maria and Jason, looked up from their work, curiosity lighting their faces. "Have you been to the market, Professor Appleby?" Maria asked. "In Mexico, where I come from, the woman of the house always takes a basket to town when she wants to buy groceries."

"No," the old man breathed again, his voice barely audible, "there are no groceries in here."

Jason tilted his head to one side, thought lines creasing his smooth, dark skin. "I'll bet that's where you carry your tools, isn't it? If you see something that needs fixing, you just whip out a hammer or screwdriver and get to work."

Professor Appleby carefully placed the basket on a nearby table. "No tools in here either," he said. "But I don't want you to look inside until after we've heard the first tape. Then you'll understand. Agreed?"

The three children nodded slowly, unsure of why their friend didn't want them to peek into the mysterious basket now resting so close by. They also wondered whether they'd be able to restrain themselves one minute longer. But they'd agreed, and Stacey, Maria, and Jason were 10-year-olds who kept their word, no matter how hard it was at times.

After Professor Appleby had left the room, the three tried to return to their work, but every so often each would glance across at the basket resting on the table and sigh.

"I hate when this happens," Jason said, trying to concentrate on the poster he was designing. "A kid's gotta know stuff.

The professor's basket is driving me crazy."

Maria bent low over her poster and applied some yellow paint to the hand-drawn outline adorning one of the corners. "I like mysteries," she said excitedly. "They make me all tingly inside."

Stacey nodded, carefully forming big letters across the top of her creation. "Grandfather is always running around trying to get me to figure out something or other. I think it's kind of a hobby. Maybe it's because he used to be a schoolteacher. They think if you don't learn something every 10 minutes the world will end."

Her two companions giggled. "And how 'bout his sister Maggie B?" Maria chimed in. "She's always digging in the ground somewhere in the Middle East trying to figure out which civilization lived there and what everyone had for breakfast 3,000 years ago. Then she sends the professor boxes and boxes of really cool stuff. I guess when or if she ever decides to come back home, she'll remember where she's been by just looking around the mansion."

"I like Maggie B," Jason sighed. "She's nice."

"How do you know?" Stacey asked. "You've never seen her."

"Don't have to," the boy stated. "I know what she's like from listening to her cassette tapes. Her voice sounds like it's smiling. And when she tells those Bible stories, I can almost see what she's talking about."

"Yeah," Maria nodded. "And speaking of story tapes, we'd better get our posters finished before the others arrive. It's a nice day, so we should have a good crowd."

Stacey held her large, thick piece of art board out in front of her, studying it carefully. "But when this happens," she stated, pointing at the painstakingly drawn letters filling the center of the design, "we won't have to worry about crowds anymore. *Everyone* can hear Maggie B's stories, no matter where they are."

Maria and Jason hurried over to her side and gazed approvingly at the words printed on the poster.

Hear Ye, Hear Ye.
Beginning Monday
listen to the famous Maggie B tapes

1

over radio station WPRL
At 4:30 p.m. sharp.
Sponsored by
the community college and
Professor Appleby's Museum of Really Old Stuff.
Be sure to tune in!"

"I like it," Maria said, nodding her head enthusiastically. "It's very professional."

"And I especially like the roses," Jason declared, motioning toward the flowers at each corner. "Makes it pretty."

"I wanted to give the impression that her stories are colorful and interesting, like bouquets of flowers," Stacey said. Laying her poster down on the table so the paint could dry, she turned toward Maria. "What artwork are you using?"

"I put clouds all around my words," her friend announced. "You know, Maggie B's voice will be going out over the airwaves, sorta like clouds drifting across the sky."

"Terrific!" Stacey beamed. "What a great idea! How 'bout you, Jason? What did you put around your words?"

The boy hesitated. "I'm not that good an artist, so I drew the only thing I know how to draw."

"And what's that?" Maria asked.

"Fruit."

"Fruit?"

He nodded. "Yeah. You know, apples, oranges, a banana. Miss Bowmen taught us how to paint fruit in art class last year. Remember?"

A smile lifted the corners of Stacey's mouth. "But what's fruit got to do with Maggie B's stories?"

"That's all I know how to draw," Jason pressed. "Unless you think I should put airplanes dropping bombs all over my poster. I'm pretty good at airplanes."

Maria giggled. "I think fruit is a much better choice." She brightened. "We can put your poster up at the grocery store. That way fruit will fit right in. Everyone will think you did it on purpose."

"I *did* do it on purpose," the boy frowned. "Just because I can't

draw flowers and clouds doesn't mean my poster was an accident. You think my hand slipped and suddenly there was a bunch of grapes in one corner? Give me a break."

"I didn't mean to make fun of your painting," Maria apologized. "What I meant to say was it'll look like you made your poster specifically for the grocery store window." The girl paused. "Hey, Jason, what kind of fruit is that down there at the bottom? It looks kinda weird."

"Oh, that?" the boy laughed. "It started out as a pineapple. Then I dripped some blue on it, so I figured I'd make it into a prune. Then the colors sorta ran together and turned it into a watermelon. As it dried, it began to look like a really big kiwi. So I just added some other stuff, and now it's just right."

"But," Maria asked, scratching her head, "what is it?"

"Fruit salad," her companion announced triumphantly.

Stacey suppressed a grin. "And a very nice fruit salad at that. Makes me hungry just looking at it."

Jason beamed. "Miss Bowmen said I have hidden talent."

The chiming of the doorbell interrupted the kitchen conversation, sending the three budding artists scurrying out of the room. Soon Professor Appleby's big den bulged with children as the afternoon storytime arrived.

"Settle down, everyone," the old man called, lifting his hands and smiling at his guests. "And welcome once again to . . . to . . ." The old man blinked. "Where exactly are we?"

Stacey's hand shot to her mouth, hiding her grin. "We're at your big house in the clearing by the river, Grandfather," she called. "And all these kids have come out to listen to your sister, Maggie B, tell stories."

"Is Maggie B here?" the professor gasped.

"No. She's in the Middle East, digging in the sand, looking for ancient artifacts."

"She doesn't have to do that," the old man countered. "Got plenty of them right here in my house. See?" He pointed at the carefully arranged shelves and display cases lining the room.

"Those are the things she sent you," Stacey said patiently. "Sometimes you forget what's going on. But that's OK. I'll remind you. We'll all remind you."

Professor Appleby laughed. "And that's why the community college turned my downstairs into a museum, so folks could come out and see all the things my sister sent." He winked at her. "Fooled you, Stacey, didn't I?"

His granddaughter smiled and nodded. "And you have something in the kitchen you wanted to bring in before the story begins, right?"

"Indeed I do," the old man called, heading toward the door. "Be back in a jiffy."

While he was gone, Stacey, Maria, and Jason took their usual places at the front of the room by the tape recorder. "As you know," Stacey said, looking out over the crowded gathering, "this will be our last meeting here at my grandfather's house. Too many kids want to hear the stories. There's just not room enough anymore. And also, school is about to begin." Groans filled the high-ceilinged chamber. "So Mr. McDonald at the radio station said he would put Maggie B's stories on the air each afternoon at 4:30. That way, anyone with a radio can hear the tapes right in their car or in their bedroom or wherever they happen to be after school.

"Also, my grandfather's museum is so popular, and Maggie B keeps sending so much stuff, that the college has decided to raise funds to build a wing onto one of their buildings so these really old artifacts can be kept where they'll be safe, and my grandfather can have his home back again." Heads nodded about the room. "But the college needs money to build the wing, and Dr. Morrison, the president, says we can help if we want to. So listen carefully on the radio each afternoon. Jason, Maria, and I will come up with some ideas and let you know what's going on. OK?"

"OK!" everyone responded enthusiastically.

Professor Appleby returned from the kitchen, the basket tucked under his arms. "You're going to have to be quiet while my sister tells her story. Don't want to disturb what's in here."

Eyes opened wide as he laid the wicker object by the door. "Just listen to the story, and we'll have a peek inside later," the old man said.

Jason closed his eyes. The basket. He hadn't thought about it since leaving the kitchen. Now, here it was again, calling to him, tantalizing him with its mystery. What strange and wonderful secret waited inside? What exotic treasure had Professor Appleby tucked in the dark confines of the puzzling container? It was no use trying to figure it out. He'd have to wait along with everyone else in the room. While he might be able to draw a pretty good cantaloupe, patience was definitely not one of his talents.

Stacey slipped a tape into the machine and pressed the play button. Turning to the assembled crowd, she announced, "This one is called 'Baby in a Basket.'"

Everyone, including Stacey, blinked, casting a quick glance at Professor Appleby's mysterious object resting by the door. It couldn't be. It just couldn't be.

Suddenly the warm, friendly voice of Maggie B filled the room. Whatever was hiding in the basket would have to wait a few minutes more.

⚔ ⚔ ⚔

A new Egyptian pharaoh paced back and forth, his black brows drawn together in an ugly scowl. "Those Hebrews!" he hissed between clenched teeth. "They squat along the Nile like frogs, more of them every day. Who knows what evil they plan against the throne? Who knows what dark plots they hatch with my enemies? But I, the great pharaoh, god of Egypt, will stop them!"

A court official watched nervously as the king paced and raved. Ever since it had thrown out the Asiatic kings who had conquered them centuries before, Egypt had distrusted foreigners, but this king's hatred of Jacob's descendants went beyond reason. It smacked of madness.

With a wild look in his eyes, the king continued. "Who gave these people the right to use some of the best land in Egypt without paying taxes on it, anyway? Who . . .?"

His official interrupted. "It seems, Your Majesty, that a certain Joseph, a Hebrew, was once prime minister here and—"

"I don't want to hear it! There are more Hebrews than Egyptians in Egypt now!" Pharaoh thundered. And no one dared correct his exaggerated claim. "Before they join with our enemies against us, we will make them slaves. Egypt will no longer pay them for their work in the fields and mines."

Later, as Pharaoh inspected Egypt from his boat on the Nile, he smiled as he saw the Hebrews bending over crops in the blazing sun. They worked hard, but sometimes he saw the slave drivers' whips lashed across their bare backs. Although the Hebrews staggered under heavy loads of copper ingots and building stone, sometimes fainting in the heat, he did nothing. Pharaoh watched as they stood knee-deep in mud, making thousands of bricks while mosquitoes and gnats swarmed over their tired bodies. He showed no pity as Hebrew slaves, sweating and trembling, loaded and unloaded giant slabs of limestone and granite from the barges on the Nile.

It's working! he thought. *With the sweat of these slaves I will build great cities, vast grain silos, temples, and monuments. And hundreds will die under the sun and the whip!* But as the months and years dragged by, Pharaoh's smile faded. His inspection of the land of Egypt revealed more Hebrews than ever. He had no idea that the God of Jacob blessed and multiplied them, as He had promised. "This is impossible!" he raged. "The more we oppress these Hebrews, the more they increase and spread!" One day he turned to his aide, a deadly gleam in his eye. "Send for the Hebrews' head midwives," he directed in a voice that chilled even the coldhearted official.

The chief midwives, Shiphrah and Puah, bowed before Pharaoh. The words he spoke sickened them.

"I command you to kill all the newborn baby boys of the Hebrew women when you help them give birth. Now go!"

The two women looked at each other. Together they determined to disobey the king.

Months later Pharaoh paced like a caged lion. A blue vein stood out and throbbed on his forehead. Shiphrah and Puah cowered before him. "Didn't I command you to kill the baby boys of those Hebrew women? Why do I see more and more of them, everywhere sprouting like reeds?" he screamed.

"The Hebrew women are very strong," the midwives answered fearfully. "Many of them have their babies without our help."

Pharaoh thought of the Hebrew women he had seen in the fields, picturing their strong brown arms. He remembered their bent backs, often burdened with a small child tied to them as the women worked all day under the scorching sun. *It must be true!* he concluded.

Dismissing the midwives, he called for his most trusted servant. "Proclaim this throughout the land of Egypt," he barked. "Let the newborn girls of the Hebrews live, but take all the boy babies and throw them into the Nile!"

In the Hebrew villages the news spread like fire in a field of stubble. Mothers and fathers rocked back and forth, overwhelmed with grief and fear. *Oh, God of our people, where are You?* they thought. *Here we are, slaves in a foreign land. The Egyptians have taken our freedom and our dignity. Will they also take our children?* The thought of helpless babies drowning in the Nile haunted them. Visions of sprawling crocodiles, suddenly springing to life to devour their children, tortured them day and night.

But some still hoped. Continuing to trust God, they remembered His promise to lead them back to the land of Canaan *after* He had made them a great nation in Egypt. Some even recalled the story of a vision God had given their ancestor Abraham—a strange vision of stars, and birds, and firepots. It told of slavery in a foreign land, but then deliverance.

Amram and Jochebed, of the tribe of Levi, did not give up hope. They believed God would send a deliverer.

Jochebed placed her hands protectively across her stomach. "Amram," she whispered. "If this child is a boy, God will protect him. I feel, somehow, that the baby born to us will be a special child."

Amram didn't know what to say, for he felt it too. But how would they keep their baby safe? Egyptian soldiers were everywhere. And now even people in the street might kill their baby. "Jochebed," he finally answered, "we must pray. Let's call Miriam and little Aaron together and ask God to take care of our baby."

Finally the new baby arrived. Jochebed cuddled the tiny form in her arms. Miriam, wide-eyed, touched the baby's soft head and gently stroked a few strands of its dark hair. Aaron tried to climb into his mother's lap to have a better look. Amram beamed with pride, but as his eyes met Jochebed's, fear mingled with love, for the new child was a boy.

Miriam spent lots of time taking care of her baby brother. *How could he sleep so much?* she wondered. But Jochebed thanked God that her baby slept and seldom cried. She could hardly think what would happen if people in the streets should hear him.

But as the baby grew, he slept less and cried more. His chunky little body grew strong, and so did his voice. At last Amram and Jochebed knew they could no longer hide him in their home. They prayed and asked God to take care of their little boy, then Jochebed called Miriam to her.

The girl looked into her mother's dark, serious eyes. "Miriam, I have made a little boat of papyrus reeds and coated it with tar so it won't leak. It has a cover that will let in air. We'll put our baby in the little boat, hide it among the tall grasses growing in the shallow water, and ask God to guard it. Perhaps He'll send a kind Egyptian woman to the river to wash clothes or bathe, and she will find my baby and care for him. But you, Miriam, must stay and watch. Let me know what happens to our baby!" Jochebed's voice broke, and she stopped speaking.

Tenderly she held her baby for what might be the last time. Kissing his chubby cheeks again and again, she finally placed him in the little basket-boat. Wiping her tears, she looked straight at Miriam. "Come," she said.

Close to the river's edge birds wheeled and called in the early-morning light. Jochebed and Miriam walked quickly, quietly, past the muddy banks where crocodiles crawled out of the water to sun themselves. Plunging into the tall reeds, mother and daughter made their way to a sheltered canal leading away from the Nile. Finally they reached a quiet pool. Breathing a prayer, Jochebed stooped and placed the little boat in the water. Then, with trembling hands, she lifted the cover for one last peek. Dark lashes brushed his rosy cheeks. Peaceful as the little pool in which he rocked, the baby slept. *But, oh,* thought Jochebed, *how long will it be before he wakes with hunger? Who will feed my baby? Who—oh, dear God, please take care of my little boy!*

With a muffled cry and a long, desperate look at Miriam, Jochebed fled.

Miriam crouched behind the reeds. The little boat rocked gently among the grasses. Hours passed, and the sun climbed higher in the sky. The heat boiled off the water, and the swarms of flies grew thicker. A whimper rose from the basket, then a cry. *Oh, what shall I do?* Miriam thought. *I'd better take him out of the basket for a little while.*

Balanced on one foot as she reached for the little boat, she froze. Voices! She heard voices . . . coming closer! She shrank back into the reeds.

Suddenly, not 20 feet away from her, stood a young Egyptian woman clothed in the finest linen. Several other women, waving ostrich fans, hovered around her. *A princess!* Miriam thought. *The pharaoh's daughter has come here to bathe!*

The baby's cries grew louder. A puzzled look crossed the princess's face; then she spotted the little boat bobbing in the lazy current. Pointing excitedly to it, she commanded, "Go get that basket for me!"

Flushed and excited, the princess bent over the basket. Eagerly lifting the cover, she looked straight into a pair of big brown eyes filled with tears.

A thousand thoughts raced through her mind. *A baby! A beau-*

tiful baby boy. It must be a Hebrew infant. Some poor woman has tried to save her child's life—and— I'll do it! I'll call this baby my own son, and he will be a prince of Egypt. This is an answer to my prayer to the goddess Hathor for a child.

Miriam had been watching, heart thudding, as the princess cuddled her baby brother. She could wait no longer. Bursting from her hiding place, she ran, splashing, to the princess.

The princess looked at her, startled. "Excuse me, Your Highness," the girl stammered, "but would you like me to find a Hebrew woman to nurse the baby for you?"

The king's daughter gave her a long look. "Yes," she said finally. "Please do."

Forgetting her bath, the princess and her maids followed Miriam back through the reeds, up the riverbank, into the narrow streets where the Hebrews crowded together along the banks of the Nile. The girl disappeared into a mud-brick hut.

Soon Miriam returned with a Hebrew woman—Jochebed. It was all the mother could do to keep from crying out and reaching

for that familiar little basket when she saw a maid holding it. But with a silent prayer for self-control, she kept her face calm as the princess spoke.

"If you will nurse this baby for me, I will pay you," the princess said. Jochebed solemnly agreed while her heart fluttered and sang like a bird. When the princess left she hugged the baby, then Miriam and little Aaron. And when Amram came home they thanked God together for bringing back their baby, the infant that the princess would call "Moses."

✗ ✗ ✗

As the story ended, all eyes turned toward the basket resting by the door. No one spoke. The only sound was the steady tick-tock of the big clock in the hallway.

Stacey removed the cassette from the machine and handed it to Maria, who placed it carefully in its plastic case. After returning the audiocassette to an empty slot in the tape case, she looked over at the professor. "Now may we see what's in the basket?"

The old man frowned. "What basket?"

"Grandfather!" Stacey laughed, pointing. "Don't tease us anymore. Please. You've gotta show us what's in there, or we'll burst."

Professor Appleby grinned from ear to ear, his nose wrinkling with the exertion. "All right, all right," he called, weaving his way around groups of seated children. "If you insist. But first, what do you think is in my basket?"

"A BABY!" the roomful of happy children sang out as in one voice.

"Well, I don't want to disappoint you, but there's not a baby in here. "To be truthful, there are *eight* babies in my basket."

Jason, who could contain himself no longer, jumped to his feet and ran to the professor. "Eight babies? They can't all fit in there."

"Oh, but they can," the old man chuckled, opening the cover and pulling out a squirming ball of fur. "They can if they're kittens!"

"Oh!" the children breathed, happy smiles lighting each face. "What beautiful kittens."

Maria grinned so hard her cheeks hurt. "Look how cute they are. When were they born?"

"Just last week," Professor Appleby stated. "Found them under my front porch. Don't know where the mother is. Been feeding them warm milk out of a doll bottle. I put a hot water bottle next to them about an hour ago so they would nap. I was afraid they'd wake up right in the middle of Maggie B's story and spoil the surprise."

Children crowded around the old man, each wanting to get a closer look at the squirming pile of tiny felines. "Do they have names?" one asked.

"Not yet," Professor Appleby said. "They will soon enough. You can help. But first I want to talk to you for a minute."

The children settled back in their places, filling every square inch of the den floor. "There was a reason I waited to show these kittens to you until after you'd heard Maggie B's story. How many of you would want to put these tiny, innocent little fellows into a floating basket and set it adrift in a river where snakes and crocodiles lived?"

"No way," a child said. "They might get hurt."

"Then think about how Moses' mother felt when she placed her tiny baby in just such a basket and gently pushed it out from the shore. Imagine how that sister felt as she watched and waited, hiding among the reeds."

"That would be very scary," another child said. "And dangerous."

"That's right," Professor Appleby agreed. "And I think God felt the very same way when He looked down on this earth and saw His children floating about in a river of sin and suffering, knowing full well that Satan was hiding just under the water, waiting to hurt us.

"So He sent His Son, Jesus, to wait among the reeds, ready to help us when danger approached." The old man paused. "We hear a lot about God the Father. But I think we should think of our heavenly parent as like a *mother* too. Don't you?"

Maria nodded. "I like that idea," she said quietly. "If God is like my mother, then He's even more wonderful than I thought."

"Yeah," Jason agreed. "I think so too."

Stacey walked over and gave her grandfather a little hug. "Thank you for that nice lesson," she whispered. "I've always thought my mom was special. Now I know why."

"So," the old man smiled, "who'd like to hold one of the kittens from my basket?"

Hands shot up. The old man nodded. He and Maggie B made a great team. Between her voice and his actions, God's love could reach anyone who took the time to listen, and learn a lesson from the past. With that thought resting comfortably in his mind, Professor Appleby listened intently as his sister's next story began.

(The activity for the story of Moses as a baby is found on page 58.)

ELIJAH FED BY RAVENS

Besides food, the ravens also brought a message to Elijah. Unscramble the letters to read the message.

___ ___ ___   ___ ___ ___ ___ ___

Why Was Pharaoh So Mad at the Hebrews?

Pharaoh's mistreatment of the Hebrews puzzles us. Why would he want to kill off their male children, his future slaves?

One of the reasons he and the Egyptians were so hostile to the Hebrews was that God's people were Asiatics, or Semites, who had migrated from the Asiatic part of the Middle East. It was a bad time to be a Semite, because the Egyptians were still smarting from the fact that Asiatics had ruled part of their country for several centuries. Having fought what they considered a long hard struggle to regain their independence and freedom, the Egyptians vowed never again to allow themselves to fall under the control of foreigners, especially the people of Palestine and Syria. Semites had become a too powerful part of the Egyptian population. This must never happen again.

How had so many Semites wound up in Egypt? For many reasons.

First, Palestine, Syria, and the lands around Egypt depended upon rainfall for agriculture. If the rains did not come at the right time and in the right amount, people faced starvation. But the Nile provided a much more regular source of moisture for farming. The Egyptians could use its water for irrigation. Thus the Nile Valley would often have food when famine swept neighboring countries, a situation we see mentioned several times in the book of Genesis.

Also, when war swept through Palestine, people fled to Egypt for refuge. In addition, the prosperous Egyptian civilization attracted droves of merchants and traders for business reasons as well as herders eyeing the fertile grazing land in the delta region. Still others came to Egypt seeking work or as slaves and captives.

As a result Egypt had a constant migration of Asiatics and other people into its territory, especially during the late Middle

Kingdom period (c. 1800-1650 B.C.) They established villages and towns along the border between the Nile Delta and Canaan. When the Egyptian royal authority declined during the Second Intermediate Period (1650-1550 B.C.), the Asiatics living in the Delta were able to take advantage of the chaos and assume control of the region. Eventually they pushed south and conquered the northern part of the Nile Valley. The Egyptians referred to these usurpers as *heka khaswt,* "rulers of foreign lands" or "desert princes," from which we get the name Hyksos. The Egyptians applied the term to any foreigners from Syria-Palestine as well as Nubia to the south of Egypt.

The Hyksos in Egypt established their capital at Avaris in the eastern Delta region. They allied themselves with the Nubians, who were at the same time invading the Nile Valley from the south. It may be during this period that Pharaoh put Joseph in power under him and invited Jacob and his family to settle in Egypt.

The Hyksos adopted Egyptian lifestyle and worshiped Egyptian gods. They introduced the widespread use of horse and chariot and new types of armor and military strategies, all of which the Egyptians soon turned against them. Even though the Hyksos tried to be like them, the proud Egyptians naturally resented their Asiatic overloads. A group of local rulers at the city of Thebes resisted the Hyksos and began to fight for Egyptian independence, forming a group of Egyptian rulers that we know today as the seventeenth dynasty.

The last leader of the seventeenth dynasty, Kamose (ruled 1555-1550 B.C.), drove the last of the Hyksos from the Delta and reestablished complete Egyptian control of the whole country. Archaeologists have excavated the beautifully decorated palaces he destroyed at Avaris (modern Tell el-Daba). The palaces had frescoes that resemble those found in Minoan palaces at Knossos on the island of Crete.

The Hyksos were probably never as ruthless as ancient Egyptian documents depict them, but they did shatter Egyptian pride and confidence. Ancient Egyptian history depicted the arrival of the Hyksos as massive hordes of invaders when in reality the Asiatics had only gradually entered Egypt over a long period of time. Regardless of what really happened, the native people of the Nile Valley determined never to let Asiatics or other foreign people threaten them again.

Once they had driven out the hated Hyksos, the Egyptians re-organized the government, made slaves of many more of the Asiatics still in the land, and built forts along the eastern edge of the Delta to keep any additional foreigners out of the country. (When Moses led the Hebrews out of Egypt, he turned south to avoid this string of fortresses and the soldiers garrisoned there.) Recognizing that they could no longer remain isolated from the rest of the world, the Egyptian pharaohs marched across the desert to create a mighty empire.

② Airwaves

Mom, I'm home." Stacey burst through the front door of the little green house on Fern Street and tossed her backpack onto the couch. "Grandfather says thank you for the new towels you sent. He thinks they look really cool in his bathroom."

Mrs. Roth, Stacey's mother, appeared briefly in the hallway as she hurried from her small home office to the kitchen, a length of fax paper fluttering behind her. She was still wearing her work clothes—a pair of carefully pressed jeans and a dark-blue sweatshirt. The woman hated dresses.

"He put those new towels in his bathroom?" she called. "They were for his kitchen. Got pictures of *vegetables* printed all over 'em. He's supposed to hang them from those little knobs on the counter doors."

The girl shrugged. "Guess he needed something for his shower. Besides, he's already got towels in his kitchen—big blue ones with sailboats and seashells all around the borders."

"*Those* were supposed to be for his bathroom," came the disembodied reply. "Sometimes I think your grandfather is as crazy as everyone says he is."

Stacey frowned. "He's not crazy. A little mixed-up, maybe."

Her mother's smiling face appeared at the entrance to the kitchen, reading glasses balanced securely at the end of her nose. "I know, I know. He's my father, and I love him. But he does tend to get—how shall I put this?—a little disorganized from time to time."

Stacey grinned. "And that's on his good days."

Disappearing down the hallway, Mrs. Roth called over her shoulder, "Why don't you start supper? I've got a little more editing to do on this story for tomorrow's edition, then I'll join you. There's a can of olives in the pantry. We can have pizza. How's that sound?"

"Sounds better if you fix it."

The woman laughed. "Next time. Promise."

Stacey nodded and sighed. Next time. Promise. Where'd she heard those words before? Maybe it was yesterday, when her mom couldn't pick her up at the community swimming pool and she had to hitch a ride home with Jason. Or was it last week, when she wanted her mother to watch a video with her and the town's mayor decided to hold a press conference down on the courthouse lawn?

The girl opened the refrigerator door and peered into the freezer section. Or was it the week before, when she just wanted someone to talk to, but Mrs. Courtney, who lived alone with nine cats, had chosen that very moment to drive her car off the Duckwall bridge into the river and had to be rescued by four fire-fighters and an old dog who did nothing but stand on the bank and howl at the moon? The phone had rung as she and her mother had settled themselves onto the couch for a rare mother-daughter chat.

Finding the box of pizza, Stacey withdrew it and stood reading the directions written on the back of the container. No, the last time she heard her mother use that line was earlier today, right before she had left for Professor Appleby's house to work on her poster. Stacey had called the town newspaper office where her mother was editor and asked Miss Putnam, the woman who answered the phone and wrote the obituaries, if Mrs. Roth could talk to her daughter for a moment. The phone line went dead for five seconds, then Miss Putnam's cheery voice returned. "Your mother can't speak with you right now," she said, her words sounding like sugar being sprinkled over cornflakes. "But Mrs. Roth told me to tell you that the next time you call, she will certainly, abso-lutely, without hesitation take a break and listen to what you, her one and only daughter, have to say. And that's a promise."

Stacey chuckled under her breath as she punched the proper sequence of numbers into the microwave's temperature/time panel and pushed the start button. Even now she could hear tick-ity-tap-tapping echoing down the hallway, indicating her mom was hard at work, writing something profound for tomorrow's edition. The townspeople depended on her and her publication.

Day after day, page after page tumbled from the smelly, ink-and oil-stained press that rattled and shook the basement walls of her mom's office building across the street from the shopping plaza. She always had a new story to write, or a lead to follow up on, or an important person to interview. Stacey's endless supply of questions would just have to wait. But she knew her mother would eventually find the time to listen. After all, she'd promised.

"Something smells yummy," the woman called from down the hall. "There's some leftover tossed salad in the fridge. You can make the dressing. Easy on the oil. Don't want to clog our arteries."

"I know," Stacey acknowledged, strolling down the passageway and pausing at the office door. Her mother was sitting at the desk across the room, her slender, energetic form leaning forward slightly, eyes scanning the glowing letters as they popped onto the screen in response to her flying fingers on the keyboard.

The girl stood and studied her mother thoughtfully, admiring how the late afternoon sun flooded through the window and washed over the woman's shoulders, illuminating her long, soft, blond hair and the gentle curve of her face. Ever since she was a child, Stacey had believed her mom to be the prettiest woman on earth with the exception of one actor she'd seen in a toothpaste commercial.

She couldn't remember her father. He'd died when she was a baby. So it had always been just the two of them facing the world together. That is, until five months ago, when Mr. McDonald, the manager of the local Christian radio station, had moved to town. Soon thereafter, Stacey had noticed her mother taking a few extra seconds at the mirror before leaving the house. New, exotic-smelling perfumes had appeared on the bathroom counter, and the musical sounds of WPRL had become a constant background in their little cozy home under the big oaks.

Mr. McDonald wasn't so bad. Stacey liked having him around. He was funny, caring, and drove a four-wheel-drive truck. It was his daughter that was the problem. Marlene. Even hearing her name was like recalling the high-pitched whine of a dentist's drill. The girl was a few months younger than she was, but to listen to Marlene talk, you'd get the impression she was 10 going on 20.

Stacey saw her mother pause and glance at some notes lying on the table. She wanted her to be happy, and if Mr. McDonald could accomplish that, fine. But *Marlene?* If her mom and the radio station manager ever decided to marry each other, Stacey had long ago planned to put herself up for adoption.

Strolling back down the hallway in response to the *beep-beep-beep* of the microwave, the girl sighed. Life. It was certainly an adventure.

Monday morning dawned bright and cool. Stacey spent the first part of the day at the local discount store, trying to pick out a new book binder and a fresh supply of pencils for all the homework and studies to come. Maria and Jason joined her there, surveying the selections and discussing the merits of each.

After eating lunch at Maria's house, the three friends hurried over to the radio station to discuss the upcoming Maggie B programs and how they could help raise funds for the museum wing at the community college. Mr. McDonald welcomed them warmly, offering his own office for a conference room.

They bantered ideas about, but most proved too expensive or just plain impossible—like Jason's brainstorm to have the Navy's Blue Angels precision flight team perform above the town.

"We don't have an airport," Stacey countered. "Besides, with all the trees lining our streets, we wouldn't even be able to watch the show."

Maria's suggestion of a bake sale drew some favorable comments, especially when she said her mother could provide a goodly supply of tostadas, a personal favorite of both Stacey and Jason. But that idea faded when the three realized that most moms were too busy to bake anything, much less participate in a sale.

"We've got to do something that doesn't take up too much time and doesn't cost a million dollars, but draws attention to the museum wing project and gets people to donate tons of money." Stacey drummed her fingers on the table. "Any more ideas?"

"Yes," Maria sighed. "Let's stop talking about this and rest our brains. I think mine is beginning to wear out."

Jason laughed. "Now, *that's* a good idea. Besides, it's almost

4:30, time for Maggie B's first story on the radio."

The three jumped to their feet and hurried down the long hall-way to the glass-walled room at the far end. Pressing their noses against the smooth surface, they watched Mr. McDonald skillfully adjust volume controls and cue up CDs and tapes.

As the hands on the big round clock above his head reached exactly 4:30, he silenced the song that was playing and an-nounced, "This is W-P-R-L, the radio voice of Valley Springs and the surrounding area. It's 4:30, time for a new feature on our sta-tion sponsored by the community college and Professor Appleby's Museum of Really Old Stuff, or the Appleby Museum of Antiquity, depending on whom you talk to." The man winked at the chil-dren, then continued. "As you know, the good professor has a sis-ter named Maggie B who's an archaeologist traveling the back roads of the Middle East, digging up ancient treasures and writ-ing stories about a time long past—stories from the Bible.

"Our adventures today center on a man named Moses and the group of people he was trying to lead to a Promised Land. So sit back, relax, and enjoy the very first broadcast of Maggie B's Radio Story Time."

The children saw Mr. McDonald reach over and press a but-ton on a cassette deck mounted in a tall rack of audio equipment by his right elbow. The speaker above their heads was silent for a moment; then a familiar voice filled the hallway and the air-waves of Valley Springs.

✗ ✗ ✗

Only a few weeks had passed since the Israelites had escaped from Egypt. Obal could still picture that great highway through the Red Sea and the mighty waters rushing and roaring as they covered and drowned the Egyptian army. But even though the people remembered God's miracles, they still didn't fully trust Him, or Moses and Aaron.

Moses called a stop to their journey, and the travelers sank wearily to the ground. Gazing around at the towering cliffs and barren, stony earth with its occasional shrub or tuft of grass, they began to complain. "Where are the fields of grain? Where are the melons and vegetables that gew in Egypt?

Moses, you have led us into the desert to die!"

Moses scanned the hordes of people spread out over the desert. *What a group!* he thought. *They have never known anything but slavery. Yet terrible as slavery was, it was familiar. Now, in spite of God's miracles, they long for Egypt!*

Dear God, he prayed, *give me wisdom and patience to guide these people. And, Lord, what shall I give them to eat?*

God quickly answered Moses' prayer. "I will cause food to rain down from the sky," He assured him. "Tell the people to gather just enough for the day early in the morning. On the sixth day they must collect twice as much as usual. In this way I will test them to find out how well they will follow My instructions."

Obal leaned forward, eager not to miss anything that Aaron was saying. "Your God has heard your complaints, and He will give you meat to eat in the evening, and in the morning you will find food that has rained down from the sky!" As Aaron spoke, the smoky cloud that guided them shone with the brilliance of God's presence. Aaron kept on talking, but Obal stared at the cloud and wondered. God would rain down food from the sky? What next would their wonderful God do for them? *I'm going to stay awake all night,* he promised himself, *so I can see the food rain from the sky.*

As the sun lowered in the west a whirring sound filled the air, and hundreds of quail flew into the camp. Joyously the Israelites raced around, casting nets over the birds. Obal spotted a fat bird sitting beside a clump of bushes. "I'll bet I could catch that bird!" he whispered. Moving quietly, slowly, he sneaked up on the tired quail. Then with a sudden rush, he threw himself to the ground, his arms encircling the squawking bird. Its feathers beat against the boy, but Obal held on tight. "I did it!" he shouted. At suppertime the Israelites feasted on quail. Obal remembered to thank God for the meal.

That night the boy lay staring into the darkness. Through his thin mat he could feel stones burrowing into his back. His brothers and sisters breathed quietly as Mother and Father talked in low voices. Once in a while the bleat of a sheep or lamb echoed in the still air. Obal's eyes grew heavy. *I won't go to sleep . . . I won't . . .*

The pale light of early morning touched his eyelids. With a

start he awakened. No one else was in the tent. "Oh!" he groaned, "I went to sleep after all!" Throwing off his wool blankets, he dashed outside. A strange sight met his eyes.

The ground, brown and barren the night before, sparkled with tiny white bits of something he had never seen. "What is it?" people asked each other.

"This is the food that the Lord has given you to eat," Moses answered. "Gather as much as you need for your families—about two quarts for each person." The people ran to get baskets, but Obal just had to have a taste. Stretching out one hesitant finger, he lifted one of the sparkling bits from the ground and brought it to his mouth. It rested sweetly on his tongue. A smile spread across his face. "Mmmm! It's good!" he murmured. "It tastes like honey, only better!"

Obal noticed that many people greedily gathered more than God had told them to. They scooped up as much of the food from heaven as they could stuff into their baskets.

In the morning wails arose from many tents. "It's spoiled, and it's got worms in it!" whined the people who had disobeyed God's instructions.

On the sixth day of the week Moses reminded them, "Today you must gather twice as much as you have on other days so that you will be ready for the Sabbath. On God's rest day He will not send food from the sky. So gather twice as much and save the extra for the Sabbath. It will stay fresh and good, but only for the Sabbath day."

Just as God had promised, the manna, as the people called it, tasted as fresh and sweet on the Sabbath as it had on the day before. Obal bit hungrily into a little cake his mother had made with the manna. "This is a gift from God, isn't it, Mother?" he asked softly. Her brown eyes sparkled. "It surely is!"

At last the Israelites broke camp and started on their way again, following the smoky cloud and the fiery pillar. The manna continued to fall every night, no matter where they were. Finally they came to Rephidim, a dry valley at the foot of a mountain, and there the people began to complain again. "How can we set up camp here, Moses? There's no water. We're thirsty. We'll all die of thirst out here in the desert, and it's all your fault. Now give us water to drink!"

"Why do you always find fault with me?" Moses asked. "Don't you realize that you're blaming God?"

But the thirst-crazed people hardly heard him. "You're going to kill us, our children, and our livestock!" they shouted. The mood grew ugly. Dark scowls and angry glares threatened Moses. Obal's heart beat fast as he watched some of the men reach for the stones that littered the ground.

Moses looked anxious. Turning his back on the people, he prayed. "Lord," he asked, "what can I do with these people? They're almost ready to stone me!"

"Take some of the leaders of Israel with you," God answered, "and go on ahead of the people. Take along the stick with which you struck the Nile. I will stand before you on a rock at the foot of the mountain. Strike the rock, and water will flow out of it for the people to drink."

Obal felt proud as he watched his father and other leaders go with Moses to a huge outcropping of rock jutting out of the side of the mountain. God's shining presence hovered over it. Holding his wooden staff high, Moses brought it down with a thwack against the stone.

Suddenly a great stream of clear, sparkling water spurted from the rock and gushed to the ground. The people rushed to the stream, burying their faces in the water, splashing it over their heads and necks. They pushed and shoved, all trying to get to the water at once.

But Moses' voice, ringing with God-given authority, brought them to attention. "Form a line!" he directed. Obal listened as their leader continued talking, making sure everyone received water—from the children and old people to every goat and lamb in the flocks.

As Obal finally leaned over the still-gushing stream, he thought, *Another gift from God—another miracle! I wonder what will happen next!*

✗ ✗ ✗

Mr. McDonald slid a control knob forward and leaned toward the microphone. "For those of you who have just joined us, you're listening to Maggie B's Story Time on W-P-R-L, the friendly, hometown voice of Valley Springs. This is Bob McDonald.

"Our next story continues the adventures of Moses and his people as they wander through the desert." He picked up a sheet of paper and read it. "This story is entitled 'The Golden Bull.' Here once again is Maggie B."

Obal scowled at his sister, Milcah. Although younger than he, she had recently grown taller, and now looked down at him with a superior air. She tossed her head, and her long black hair swirled, strands of it peeping out from under her head covering as if they had a mind of their own. *That's the trouble with Milcah!* Obal thought. *She has too much of a mind of her own, and she always thinks she's right!*

The camp was in an uproar about Moses' disappearance. Since he had entered that fiery cloud of smoke almost six weeks ago, nearly everyone felt sure he had deserted them. But not Milcah.

Two red spots flamed on her cheeks, and her eyes flashed. "I don't care what anyone says. I know Moses wouldn't just go off and leave us!"

Obal squirmed. With Milcah's blazing eyes upon him, he felt guilty for doubting Moses and doubting God. *But six weeks! Six weeks of staring at the smoky cloud as it again and again burst into flame and swirled around the mountain. Six weeks of listening to the roll of thunder without one comforting word from Moses. Six weeks of being stranded in a barren wilderness, not knowing where they were or how to get to Canaan.*

Even now Obal and Milcah could hear the complaints of many people. "Moses has led us out here into the wilderness to die. God has taken him away from us and forsaken us. Now what will we do? We need a god that we can see, a god like those of the Egyptians!"

"Do you hear that?" Milcah demanded. "After all that God has done for us, and just a few weeks after we all promised to do everything He said, and with His presence still right there on the mountain, do you hear the people saying that God has forsaken us? Well, I know He hasn't!"

Suddenly Obal knew that Milcah was right, and he felt ashamed for thinking, even for an instant, that God had let them down. But before he could say anything, the voices of the people swelled to a roar.

"Aaron! Make us a god that we can see! We don't know what has become of this Moses, who dragged us out of Egypt. Come on, Aaron; give us a god to worship!"

Little drops of sweat popped out on Aaron's forehead. *Oh, why doesn't Moses come back?* he fumed. *I can't stand up to the people like he does!*

"Uh, look," he ventured, "are you sure you really want to do this? If you could wait—"

But the people cut him off. "Make us a god that we can see and worship. Let's hold a festival like the ones we saw in Egypt."

Aaron thought fast. Maybe if he asked the people to donate their valuable jewelry to make an idol, they wouldn't want to do it. So in an easy-going voice he directed, "Everyone—men, women, children—take off your earrings and bring them to me."

His heart sank as he watched the mob of people hastily pull the earrings from their ears and rush toward him, piling the glittering gold at his feet. Out of the corner of his eye he saw that a few people held back. Most of his relatives, from the tribe of Levi, turned away from him and began to pray. A few others joined them.

He watched as a boy and girl joined the little group. The girl shot him a withering glance. Aaron felt the hot shame creep up his neck. *Little Milcah—braver than he!*

But the people were dancing around him, screaming, laughing, crying. "You have our gold; now make us a god! What are you waiting for? With Moses gone, you're in charge. Now give us what we want, or—!"

Hastily he gathered the gold jewelry and built a fire of thorn bushes and animal droppings. Using bellows, he got the fire roaring with white heat and added more and more fuel. Then he placed the gold in a crucible oven and set it over the flames. Slowly the gold began to melt, turning into a shining yellow puddle.

After waiting for the gold to cool a bit, he poured it into a clay mold that he had made. The people watched, their eyes gleaming and glittering like the fast-hardening gold itself. Aaron melted more gold. The idol began to take shape. When the mold was broken, the head of a young bull, nostrils flaring, eyes staring stupidly ahead, popped into view, followed by a body with big shoulders and spindly legs.

Setting it down carefully on a large rock, Aaron pulled together some smaller rocks, forming a rough altar. The people went wild. Now they had a priest, an altar, and an image they could see!

"Tomorrow," Aaron said, his lips feeling stiff and unnatural, "we will hold a feast day to the Lord." The words sounded right, but his stomach churned. God's words echoed in his ears: "Do not make any images. Do not worship idols." *But the people, the people!* he thought, trying to excuse himself. As he turned toward his tent he saw Milcah's eyes upon him, clear, cool, accusing.

Early the next morning the people poured from their tents like hornets from a hive. His face pale above his bushy beard, Aaron stood by the altar. "Let us worship the Lord!" he began in a shaky voice, but his words vanished in the noise and commotion. Sheep and goats bleated as men rushed among them, grabbing one here, another there, to slaughter and offer as sacrifices to the golden bull.

"This is the God who brought us out of Egypt!" the people chanted. Stuffing themselves with the remains of their sacrificed and roasted animals, they sang, laughed, and danced around the little golden object. Feeling sick, Milcah and Obal stumbled toward their own tent, not wanting to see any more of the false worship.

At the top of the mountain Moses talked with God. Having left his young soldier friend Joshua farther down the mountain, Moses listened to God, completely unaware of the passing of time. God told him to prepare a special tent for Him to dwell in as the Israelites moved from place to place. He described how the priests should dress and how to build a special altar for Him.

God's presence surrounded Moses. His glory spilled over and washed him in a dazzling white light. Moses' heart sang with the joy of being with God.

In his hands he held two large, flat rocks, given to him by God Himself. He had watched, astounded, as God, with His finger, had written the Ten Commandments on the stones. Reverently he held them, imagining how happy the people would be when they saw them.

But suddenly God's loving voice changed. Thunder boomed and lightning flashed with a fierceness not seen before, as He exclaimed, "Go down quickly to the camp. Your people have disgraced themselves. They have broken their promise to Me and made a golden bull. Worshiping it, they made sacrifices to it and have given an idol credit for delivering them out of Egypt.

"These people are stubborn and hardheaded. Don't bother to plead their case. I have a mind to destroy them all, but I will make a great nation of you and your children."

But Moses knew God well enough to know how much He loved His people. *He knows that I will plead for them!* Moses realized. *And I will, for I love these people.*

"Lord," he began, "don't be angry with Your people whom you brought so gloriously out of Egypt. Why give the Egyptians a chance to say that the God of the Hebrews took His people out into the desert and destroyed them there?

"Remember Abraham, and Isaac, and Jacob, and the promise You made to them. You promised them descendants like the stars in the sky. You promised, if they would obey You, to give them the land of Canaan forever and ever. Please give them another chance . . ." His voice trailed off, and he could think of nothing else to say.

God's heart swelled with love and pride. The baby boy He had saved from the river Nile had grown up to be a merciful, loving man.

"Return to My people," He said in a warm, low rumble.

Still clutching the two tables of stone, Moses made his way over rocks and around crevices down the mountain. At a sharp turn he caught up with Joshua. A few steps farther Joshua exclaimed, "I hear a great noise from the camp. Some tribe must have attacked, for it sounds like a battle!"

Moses knew the noises were not the sounds of warfare, but those of a wild religious celebration. Yet he was not prepared for the sight that met his eyes when he finally reached the foot of the mountain. To come directly from the presence of God into a mass of wildly dancing, idol-worshiping people was more than he could stand.

With a shout of anger he raised the sacred tables of stone above his head and threw them to the rocks at his feet. They smashed into a hundred pieces, shattered, just as the Israelites had broken their promise to obey their loving God.

The people stopped in their tracks, staring at Moses. His face shone with the dazzling light of God's presence, and his eyes flashed with anger. Dashing toward the golden idol, he knocked it into a fire and began to blow upon it with bellows. Suddenly sobered, the people watched as their wonderful little bull-god slowly melted in the flames, its stupid eyes and weak mouth running and dripping into golden puddles.

The gold cooled quickly, and Moses took the shapeless lumps, ground them into powder, and sprinkled it in the people's drinking water. "Drink!" he shouted, and the people drank, swallowing hard, wondering what terrible thing would happen to them because of their sin.

Then Moses turned to Aaron. "What did these people ever do to you, that you would turn around and make them guilty of such sin?"

Aaron's eyes darted wildly about, and he started to talk rapidly, hoping something he said would make sense. "Please don't be angry, my brother. You know these people and how set they are on doing evil. They made me do it! I didn't want to! I just took their gold and threw it in the fire, and a calf jumped out!"

Moses was too angry even to laugh at such a story. *How could he?* he asked himself over and over. *How could he do such a thing? And now he's trying to make me think it was some kind of miracle or something! O God, can You forgive such sin?*

Stepping quickly to the top of a large rock, he asked in ringing tones, "Who is on the Lord's side? Come to me!"

The descendants of Levi quickly made their way to Moses. Milcah and Obal pushed their way to the front where they could huddle against Moses and see what would happen next. "Punish those who disobeyed the Lord," he commanded, and the Levites obeyed.

The next day Moses approached the Lord and begged, "Forgive the people for making an idol. Don't blot them out of Your book of life—but if You must, blot me out too."

"I will forgive them," God answered, "but they will get sick because of their sinful actions."

Milcah and Obal strolled through the camp, quiet now except for muffled groans of illness. Obal looked thoughtfully at his sister. "I'm glad you trusted God and believed in Moses," he said. "You helped me to believe too."

Milcah tossed her head. "I'm always going to trust in God, whether grown-ups, or even Father and Mother, do. He takes care of us, and I love Him."

✗ ✗ ✗

Stacey grinned broadly as she saw Mr. McDonald lean toward his microphone. *Imagine. Maggie B's stories are no longer just being heard by a few dozen kids out at my grandfather's old mansion in the clearing. Through the electronic magic of radio, her words are flying out across the entire county, filling the valleys and hills with wonderful Bible stories. Oh, if only Maggie B could see this, she'd be thrilled!*

Stacey glanced at Maria and Jason. They too understood the wonder of what was happening. Never in their wildest dreams did they think that someday they'd be watching a man sitting in a broadcast room announce the next adventure written and read by the woman almost every child in town had come to love.

Mr. McDonald smiled as he spoke. "Our final story for today was recorded near a mountain named Horeb in the wilderness of Sinai. This is located between modern-day Egypt and the country of Israel. My notes say that Maggie B camped in a deep valley surrounded by treeless mountains and craggy rocks, not exactly the easiest place to build 'a dwelling place for God,' as our adventure is called. But that didn't stop Moses and his people from trying. Let's listen."

✗ ✗ ✗

Obal watched as Bezalel's muscular arm pulled the bronze saw back and forth, its teeth chewing their way through the hard, durable acacia wood. Then the piece of wood he had cut dropped to the ground, sending up a fine flurry of sawdust as it fell.

Bezalel wiped the sweat from his forehead and smiled at Obal. "There! That piece is just the right size for your sister's jewel box. I'll cut it up, rub the pieces with sand to make them smooth, and polish them with oil. I'll carve some designs in the wood, and then if you'll bring me that gold you promised, I'll cover the lid with pretty pictures."

Obal looked admiringly at Bezalel. The artisan's thin face with its straight nose and enormous dark eyes seemed always alight, alive, as one idea after another popped into his active mind. No one else in the whole camp could work with wood and clay and stone and make such beautiful things as Bezalel did.

"How do you do it?" Obal often asked, but Bezalel only grinned shyly and replied, "Oh, it is nothing. Anyone could do it."

But just "anyone" could not do it. Obal tried to make little clay soldiers and little wooden chariots, but his soldiers looked like lumps and his chariots resembled nothing anyone could recognize. Then Bezalel would laugh softly and hand him a handful of soldiers, each with perfectly formed features and swords and armor. Then he would give him a tiny, graceful chariot with wheels that turned, pulled by a high-stepping brass horse. Now as Obal watched a delicate jewel box for Milcah take shape in Bezalel's capable hands, he thought once more how lucky he was to have him for a friend.

Suddenly a familiar voice interrupted Obal's thoughts. "Bezalel! Bezalel! I have something important to tell you!" Moses' voice drifted toward them, and moments later Moses himself appeared.

Moses fixed Bezalel with a piercing gaze and announced, "When I was on the mountain, the Lord told me to build Him a tabernacle, a place of worship. We will carry it with us wherever we go. It must be perfect, for the Lord Himself will dwell in it. Each piece of wood must fit perfectly. Gold and silver furnishings must be fashioned with skill and care. Everything must be done exactly as the Lord has directed. And He wants you, Bezalel, to be the chief builder."

"M—me?" Bezalel stammered. "Are you sure He wants me? Surely someone older, more experienced, someone better, perhaps someone from the tribe of Levi—!"

Moses' eyes twinkled, remembering for a moment his own response to God's voice at the burning bush, but his voice was serious as he replied, "Bezalel, the Lord called you by *name*. Did you think He gave you such gifts only to make toys and jewel boxes? He has blessed others with talent, too, and named Aholiab of the tribe of Dan to assist you.

"Meet me this evening after our worship, and I will tell you all the plans the Lord has revealed to me." With that, Moses turned and strode away, his robe billowing behind him.

In the days to come, Bezalel seemed to be everywhere at once. Usually shy and quiet, he now spoke with gentle authority, organizing everyone in the camp to help with the work of building God's tabernacle.

Milcah sat with a circle of girls and women bent over three different kinds of animal skins and mounds of linen cloth. She stirred a jar of purple dye, swirling the liquid around and around. Other pots held blue dye and red dye. Smiling, eyes dancing, she held up her purple hands for all to see. "Milcah!" Mother said sharply, "we are here for work, not play!"

The girl hung her head, but a little smile still danced around her mouth. The colors were so pretty! The tabernacle would look beautiful with an inner roof of blue, purple, and scarlet linen, and three outer roofs of soft skins.

Obal helped to carry and melt the piles of gold and silver ornaments the people had carried from Egypt and eagerly given to God. His ears strained to hear Bezalel's comments and explanations. "The tabernacle will be 30 cubits long, about the length of a dozen goats strung out one behind the other. It will have two main rooms. We will call the larger, outer room the holy place and the inner room the Most Holy Place, where God Himself will dwell.

"A curtain of red, blue, and purple will separate the rooms from each other, and the women will weave threads of gold throughout the curtain, in the design of angels—like this."

Obal stared as Bezalel quickly took a golden thread and wove it in and out of a piece of cloth. When he finished, a shining angel clung to the fabric. "Here," Bezalel grinned at Obal, "take this to your mother and ask her to use it as a pattern." Obal ran, passing his father and other men as they busily sawed the slender trunks of the acacia trees.

Weeks passed, then months. At last everything was finished. Solemnly four men slipped rods through golden rings at each of the four lower corners of the "ark of the covenant," and carried it into the Most Holy Place. The ark, a small wooden chest completely covered in gold, provided a resting place for two brand-new tables of stone with the Ten Commandments on them. Bezalel had carved two cherubim covered with gold. Atop the golden lid of the ark they stood facing each other with outstretched wings. The shining lid became the mercy seat, the place where God's presence hovered, promising forgiveness of sins.

Soon others stepped forward to move the other furniture into the tabernacle. A table for bread, built from acacia wood and overlaid with gold, displayed a finely carved little golden railing around the top, to keep the bread from falling off. Golden bowls for drink offerings were placed on the table, along with golden cups for holding incense. Every Sabbath the table received fresh stacks of bread, a thank offering to God.

Next they moved the golden altar of incense into the tabernacle. God wanted His people to let their prayers constantly rise like the sweet smoke of the burning incense.

Milcah's eyes shone as someone carried the beautiful golden lampstand into the holy place. *Was anything ever more beautiful?* she wondered. Delicately carved lilies gleamed on each of its seven branches. Its light made her think of God and reminded her that He wanted His people to be a light for Him.

In the large courtyard surrounding the tabernacle men placed the bronze-covered altar for burnt offerings, and just beyond it, before the entrance to the holy place, they set a special washstand. "That's for the priests. They will wash themselves there each time they enter the tabernacle, to show that God wants His people to be clean inside and out," someone whispered.

Finally everything was in place. The tabernacle stood apart from other dwellings, soft furs draped over its gold-covered wooden frame. Bezalel, eyes glistening, thought, *What an honor! There stands the dwelling place of God, and He chose me to help build it for Him!*

Solemn excitement filled the air as Moses stepped in front of the crowd. A smile flashed across his dark face as he looked first at the tabernacle, then at the waiting people. Taking a flask of oil, he sprinkled some on each part of the tabernacle and its furnishings, dedicating it to the Lord.

Then the shining white cloud of God's presence descended over the tabernacle, and the people knew that He was pleased with them and their work. The people bowed low before God, happy and grateful that He still loved them and chose to dwell with them.

"And now," Moses finally spoke, "I would like Aaron and his sons to step forward. God has chosen Aaron's family to be His priests."

Milcah gasped as Moses reached into a basket and lifted out the special clothes for Aaron, the high priest. A golden breastplate with two enormous, shining stones on either side flashed before her eyes. Then she saw a sleeveless robe of fine white linen and a gold, blue, red, and purple outer robe with tinkling golden bells and delicate pomegranates sewn along its hem. The robes for Aaron's sons were almost as beautiful.

Aaron and his sons slipped into the gorgeous robes, then donned pure white turbans. Milcah had been told that Aaron's turban had a golden sign that said "Holiness to Yahweh." She looked at the shining white cloud, the gleaming tabernacle, and the special priestly clothes, and thought, *Surely our God is holy, worthy of a beautiful place in which to dwell!*

✂ ✂ ✂

As the broadcast ended, Stacey, Maria, and Jason smiled through the glass window at their friend. The man started a record, flooding the hallway with soothing music. Stepping from the control booth, he greeted his in-studio audience of three.

"Hi, guys," he said, a big grin lighting his face. "How'd you like the show?"

"It was great!" Jason said.

"Fantastic," Maria added.

"I hope lots and lots of kids listened," Stacey grinned.

"I'm sure they did, thanks to the terrific advertising you guys have done. I especially like the poster at the grocery store. Someone sure knows how to draw fruit."

Jason blinked. "You like it? Really?"

"Sure do," Mr. McDonald stated firmly. "It's truly a work of art." He winked at Stacey. "Someone has a promising future in the art world, that's all I can say."

Jason smiled until it seemed his face would break in two. "Thanks, Mr. McDonald. *I* made that poster. I'm glad you noticed it."

"Noticed it? Why, after seeing all that beautiful artwork, I ran right into the store and purchased a bag of apples and a whole bunch of grapes. Couldn't even help myself!"

Jason blushed. "Miss Bowmen taught me how to paint. She said I had potential."

"Well, she's certainly right. With a little more practice you could be a regular Rembrandt." Turning to Stacey, the man snapped his fingers. "Oh, that reminds me. I'll bring some of those grapes over for supper tonight. Your mother has invited us."

"Us?" Stacey asked, suddenly finding she had to prop up her smile with her cheek muscles.

"Marlene and I. We'll be there around 6:00. Marlene's looking forward to spending the whole evening with you."

Stacey nodded slowly, her smile still frozen on her face. "Great. I'll . . . I'll see you then." With a wave she and the others headed down the long hallway. At the door Maria whispered, "You can stop smiling now."

Stacey's face fell into a gloomy frown. "Oh, brother. A whole evening with Marlene. I can hardly wait."

The three exited the radio station and walked out into the late summer evening.

GOD'S LOVE REBUS

First identify each picture. Then subtract the letters as indicated. Unscramble the letters left to find three things God sent to show the Israelites that He cared about them.

_ _ _ + _ _ _ _ _ + _ _ _ _ _

- _ _ _ _ - _ _ _ _ - R

_ _ _ _ _ + _ _ _ _ + _ _ _ _

- _ _ _ - _ _ _ - E

_ _ _ _ + _ _ _ + _ _ _

- _ _ _ - _ _ _

③
Marlene

Why, Stacey Roth, it's a wonderful pleasure to see you. You're looking simply radiant. I wasn't aware that kind of sweater was back in style."

"Hello, Marlene."

So began the two girls' evening conversation. Mr. McDonald and his daughter arrived right on time. Marlene's carefully combed and braided brown hair framed her clear blue eyes and rosy cheeks. Her natural ruby-red lips, pulled back into a smile, revealed teeth any dentist would be proud of. She wore a lemon-yellow jumper over a white blouse with skillful stitching and shiny gold buttons. If there was a wrinkle on any of her clothes, Stacey couldn't see it, no matter how hard she looked.

"I had a terrible day," the visitor sighed as she and Stacey ambled down the hallway toward the back bedroom. "Right off the bat I chipped a nail. See?" She held up five soft, well-manicured fingers. Stacey noticed a tiny hairline scratch on the smallest one. "It about drove me crazy until I had it fixed."

"You had it fixed? You had a chipped nail fixed?"

Marlene blinked. "Well, of course. Doesn't everyone? Mrs. Drew at the beauty parlor did it for me. She's very good. Does my hair once a week too. Do you like it?" The girl patted her coiffure tenderly. "Cost Bob a fortune."

"Bob? Who's Bob?"

"Bob McDonald. You know, my father."

"You call your dad Bob?"

"Well, that's his name, isn't it?"

Closing her eyes, Stacey sighed. It was going to be a long evening.

Entering the room with its well-lived-in look, the two girls settled themselves on Stacey's beanbags and sat staring at each

other. After a moment Marlene glanced about, her gaze falling on a strange object lying on her host's dresser.

"What's that?" she asked.

Stacey shrugged. "It's a hand mirror."

"But," Marlene gasped, "it looks old and battered."

"Well, you would too if you'd been lying in the ground since the first century before Christ."

"What?"

Stacey stood and walked across the room. "It's a Roman hand mirror," she said, grinning at her reflection in the polished side of the object. "See? This is where you look, and the other side has a carving of a woman with her hair all done up fancy. It's supposed to have a handle right here, but Maggie B couldn't find it."

"You mean that lady on the radio?"

Stacey nodded. "Oh, you listened to the stories today?"

Marlene cleared her throat. "I usually keep my radio tuned to the classical station, but I just happened to hear a portion of the program. Very quaint, if you're into childish dramas."

"Yeah, well," Stacey smiled inwardly, "Maggie B sent this mirror to my grandfather, you know—Professor Appleby—and he's letting me keep it for a few days. Then it has to go back to the museum." She blushed. "The professor said my great beauty deserved to be reflected in only the most exquisite mirror."

Marlene tittered, her hand waving weakly out in front of her. "Grandfathers. They do flatter, don't they, no matter how undeserving we may be?"

Stacey's smile faded. "Yeah. Don't they?"

"So," Marlene said, looking around with simulated interest, "have you anything else in here that Maggie B dug up for you?"

"No, just the mirror," Stacey responded.

"I must say I'm impressed with your dedication to your grandfather and his globe-trotting sister. From what I heard, ol' man Appleby is kinda . . . well . . ."

"Kinda what?"

Marlene leaned forward slightly. "Some say he's dangerous," she whispered.

"Oh, they do, do they?" Stacey said. "Well, they're wrong. He wouldn't hurt a flea."

Marlene nodded. "You know, that's exactly what I told them."

"I'll bet you did."

"Just yesterday someone mentioned Professor Appleby's name in a conversation and I stated then and there that he's a fine and noble man who is generous of heart and sound of mind."

"You're a real pal," Stacey responded without emotion.

"And," her visitor continued, "if there is anything I can do to be of assistance to Professor Appleby or his sister, you must not hesitate to ask for my . . . uh . . . assistance."

Stacey sighed. "Well, as long as you brought it up, there is something my friends and I are trying to figure out."

"There is?"

"Yes. We need to raise money for the community college. They want to build a wing onto one of their buildings for a museum of antiquity. It would be a dream come true for Maggie B. But Maria, Jason, and I can't seem to come up with any good ideas."

Marlene thought for a moment. "How about a parade?"

"A what?"

"A parade. You know—floats, marching bands, clowns, the works. Bob organized one last year in Florida where we used to live. Raised money for AIDS research. It was a wonderful success."

"This is Valley Springs, not Miami," Stacey stated.

"So, have a Valley Springs-sized parade. Get volunteers to help, have the high school band learn a few tunes, and build a float or two. Piece of cake."

Stacey edged forward on her beanbag. "What about stuff like advertising, promotion, prizes, special guests, speakers, crowd control?"

"Crowd control in Valley Springs?"

"Oh, yeah. Not a big problem."

Marlene spread her hands. "Besides, you've got the community college behind you. After all, the money is going straight to them. Just come up with a plan and present it. They'll at least listen to what you have to say."

Stacey blinked in amazement. "Why, Marlene McDonald, you may be onto something here. A parade to raise money for the museum wing. That's a great idea."

The visitor glanced down at her toes. "Of course, any good parade needs a queen to lead the festivities. Don't you think?"

Stacey grinned from ear to ear. "If this idea flies, you can be queen, king, or ambassador to Taiwan—I don't care." She jumped to her feet. "I've gotta call Maria and Jason. They're gonna love this. I'll set up a meeting for tomorrow afternoon at the radio station. Wanna come?"

Marlene shrugged. "Sure, if you think I can help."

"Oh, this is great." Stacey beamed. "Excuse me while I run to the living room to make my calls. Thanks, Marlene."

Stacey fled the room, leaving Marlene seated alone on her beanbag chair. Slowly Marlene rose and walked to the dresser. Picking up the ancient mirror, she gazed at her dim reflection in the ancient metal. "Queen Marlene," she whispered excitedly. "Everyone will see me leading the parade. Bob will be so proud."

"This is WPRL, the hometown voice of Valley Springs. It's 4:30."

Mr. McDonald adjusted one of the volume controls on the broad audio panel spread out at his elbow and spoke into the microphone. "Today we journey to a town where, in Maggie B's words, 'the citizens still gather at the well in the evening and donkey hooves clatter over cobblestone streets and alleys.'

"She goes on to say, 'This small village sits on a hillside overlooking the blue Mediterranean, its buildings huddled together in the warm afternoon sun. Today talk is filled with politics and gossip. But more than 2,000 years ago one theme came from the lips of the people of Zarephath—their country's deadly famine.'

"With that introduction, we begin today's broadcast of Maggie B's Story Time on WPRL. Her first adventure is entitled 'Black Birds and a Brave Prophet.' So children of all ages, sit down and listen to the star of our show, Maggie B."

☒ ☒ ☒

Thin and strong as a leather strap, a sunbaked man burst into Israel's throne room and aimed his piercing gaze at the startled king. His voice rang out like a blast from a ram's horn. "As the Lord, the God of Israel, lives, there will be neither dew nor rain in the coming years until the Lord gives the word!"

Then, with a swish of his camel's hair robe, he was gone.

The air throbbed with silence. Court officials stared at the open doorway as if the man's shadow still trembled on the threshold. Servants gawked at the king and queen, wondering what would happen next.

Jezebel recovered first and, shaking with anger, screamed, "Who—was—THAT?"

Ahab's face was white with fear mingled with rage. But he took a twisted kind of pleasure in telling her the man's name.

"He's called—Elijah!"

It took only a moment for Jezebel to understand. *Elijah!* The name meant "Yahweh is my God"!

Jezebel leaped to her feet, her eyes blazing with fury. "How dare he march in here and challenge my gods?" she shouted. "How dare he insult Baal, the god of the storm, who brings dew and rain? How dare he show his Yahweh-worshiping face to us?"

Jezebel motioned to the guards. "Find that prophet of Yahweh!" she roared to all within earshot. Soon every hill and valley in Israel crawled with soldiers, guards, and palace officials, all searching for Elijah.

But God was watching over His brave messenger. "Go to the brook Cherith," He told him. "I'll take care of you there."

And unseen by his enemies, Elijah ran toward the place God had prepared for him. His escape route led him across the Jordan, high into the mountains, and into a ravine protected on all sides by steep cliffs and caves. At last he reached the wadi called the brook Cherith. The gentle sound of gurgling water welcomed him as it flowed over its bed of stones. A quick glance revealed a cave that would be his home. With a grateful sigh he lay on his back, arms folded under his head, and gazed into the blue sky. In spite of his danger, he felt at peace, for he knew that God was with him.

For years he had watched in shock as God's people, fascinated by idol worship, forgot the God who loved them. So when God called him to deliver His message, he was ready.

A sudden movement in the branches caught his eye. Then a big raven, fluttering its blue-black wings, dropped from the tree onto the ground and strutted about. Elijah idly wondered what the scavenger bird was up to. He certainly had no food for it.

The sun sank in the western sky, flooding the heavens with rosy light. And Elijah, trusting in God's care, entered his cave, closed his eyes, and went to sleep.

In the morning he awoke to the raspy, raucous cries of a dozen ravens. The prophet sat up, smiling sleepily at the noisy birds. Suddenly he sensed something strange. At first he could not name whatever it was that somehow felt wrong with this morning. Then his eyes opened wide as he sucked in his breath. He knew what it was.

No dew had fallen throughout the night! Usually the ground would be soaked with heavy dew. Dew watered the plants every night. But not this morning. Just as He had said, God had begun to reveal His power over the dew and the rain. He was showing His disloyal people that He, not Baal, held the forces of nature in His hands.

Full of wonder at God's power, Elijah knelt by a small pool, drank deeply of the cool water, then washed his hands and face. "Now, if I only had something to eat," he murmured.

Hardly had Elijah finished speaking when the ravens took to the sky with a flurry of wings. "Hmmm. Guess I scared them away," he mumbled, sorry to see them go.

But in no time they were back. And far from being afraid, they swooped to the ground and marched boldly up to the prophet. Their bright, beady eyes never left him as they came closer and closer. Elijah stared at them. He had never before seen birds behave like this.

"Say! What do you have in your mouths?" he suddenly asked the big black birds. To his astonishment, he saw that each of them carried something in its beak.

Then they were at his feet and, lowering their heads, they dropped something from their beaks. Sudden, grateful tears sprang to Elijah's eyes, for each raven had brought a morsel of food. Knowing that the same God who commanded the dew also directed the birds, he whispered, "Thank You, Lord, for this miracle. Thank You for my food!"

The weeks flowed into months. The months slid into a year, then two, then more. Not a cloud dotted the sky in all that time. Not a drop of rain fell. No blanket of dew moistened the dry land. Streams dried up. The soil turned to dust and darkened the air with each gust of wind. Trees stood leafless, their black skeletons like grim prophets of starvation. Animals bleated and lowed from hunger. Children cried for more food, while their parents turned away from them to hide the tears in their own eyes.

But Israel still did not admit its dependence upon God as the sender of rain and the giver of all good gifts. Ahab felt deep in his soul that God was punishing him and his kingdom for their idol worship. But he stubbornly refused to change his ways.

Jezebel, however, screamed at all her subjects that they had somehow displeased Baal. The god was angry with them, she claimed, and that was why no rain fell. Against all reason, she also blamed Elijah for the devastating drought, and never tired in her efforts to find and kill him. Her guards searched in every village and home but could discover no trace of him.

The prophet remained hidden in his cave beside the dwindling trickle of water. Each day God's black-feathered servants brought him enough food to survive.

But the day came when mud around the seep of water dried up and cracked. Even holes Elijah had dug deep in the mud were dry. Dust and weeds blew into the dry streambed. "What now, God?" Elijah asked, knowing full well that God must have another wonderful way of taking care of him.

And He did. "Say goodbye to the ravens, Elijah," God directed. "You're going on a journey."

51

⚔ ⚔ ⚔

Mr. McDonald checked his script and slid the microphone's volume control forward two inches. "Wait! That's only the beginning. We've yet to venture into a village where an amazing miracle is about to take place. Stay with us. But first, here's a word from our contributor, the community college of Valley Springs."

As a recorded voice began extolling the virtues of higher education, Mr. McDonald slipped out of the control room and hurried down the hallway. At the door to his office he paused. Yes, Stacey and her friends were still in there, deep in excited debate over something about a marching band. He could hear Marlene's soft voice interrupting with thoughts of her own.

The man smiled. Whatever great plans they were making must be taking all of their attention. They hadn't even come out to listen to the broadcast. It didn't matter. They could stop by Professor Appleby's mansion anytime and hear the stories on their own. For now, it looked like important stuff was going on in his office.

Quickly returning to the broadcast booth, he settled himself in his chair just as the prerecorded community college promotional tape ended.

"And now," he said, "let's return to Elijah's time and discover what's waiting for him in the small town perched above the sea. Ladies and gentlemen, boys and girls, here is Maggie B."

⚔ ⚔ ⚔

Elijah stood on the bank of the wadi, his face tilted toward the sky—listening. No longer did he hear the sound of birds or insects, for the brook Cherith had dried up. He heard no rustling of leaves, for the trees were bare and the reeds were brown. In all this scorched and thirsty land he heard just one thing—God's voice.

"Go at once to Zarephath," God said, "and stay there. I have commanded a widow in that place to supply you with food."

Elijah's heart beat a little faster. God's directions were clear, but it was a long trip, over mountains and into deep valleys. He was to go to Zarephath—a town far to the north, deep in Phoenician country, Jezebel's territory! And Jezebel, the Phoenician princess, now wore the queenly crown of Israel. It was she who had sent him into hiding, and she who had sworn she would not rest until she saw him dead. And now God was sending him into a kingdom ruled by Jezebel's own father.

But it took only a moment for Elijah to realize that Phoenician territory would be the last place Jezebel would expect to find him. He threw back his head and laughed out loud to the empty sky. Elijah had the feeling that he and God were partners, playing a trick on the foreign queen and Israel's idol-worshiping king, Ahab.

Praying all the way, he hiked over the mountains and through deep valleys. As he made his slow way toward Zarephath, he often spotted roaming bands of palace guards. Elijah had no doubt they were still searching for him. At last he sighted the Sea of Galilee. Its waters were low, and dead fish lay on its rocky shores. Once past the lake, he veered to the northwest, toward the sea, toward the coastal town of Zarephath.

Finally he reached its huge stone gates. Elijah frowned as he gazed at the deserted streets. Where were the people? Then he understood. Zarephath was a manufacturing town, a producer of pottery. But the drought he had predicted stretched east and west, north and south. And it included Zarephath. People barely able to find enough food to survive could not afford to buy new pots. The potters' yards and kilns were stacked with unsold bowls, jugs, and water jars.

But he had not come to Zarephath to look at pottery shops. He had come to find the widow who would give him food according to God's promise. Slowly he turned around, looking everywhere. A few goats straggled along the road. A man rode a donkey at a slow, sad pace. Here and there children played in the dust. Women appeared briefly in their doorways, then ducked back into the shadows.

How will I ever find the woman God told me about? Elijah asked himself.

Then a figure caught his eye. Close to the town gate, not far from him, a woman bent among the dry grass and withered weeds, searching the ground for twigs. Praying with every step, Elijah approached her. When he was quite near, he asked, "Would you please bring me a little water in a jar so that I might have a drink?"

The woman looked up, startled. Who was this stranger who dared ask for water in the middle of a drought? She glanced at Elijah's worn sandals and dusty clothes and knew he had traveled far. His accent told her that he was an Israelite from the land where people worshiped Yahweh. For a second she hesitated. Water was precious. Yet how could she refuse? The law of hospitality demanded that she give him a drink.

Managing a smile, she nodded and turned toward the well, its water level dangerously low. But she had gone only a few steps when Elijah called, "And bring me, please, a piece of bread."

The woman stopped in her tracks, turned slowly, and stared at him, her dark eyes filled with distress. *Bread! The man wants bread!* she told herself, teetering on the edge of hysteria. She thought of her son and his thin little body. As she had left her home, his cries had followed her with nearly the same words: "Bring me some bread, Mother!"

With an effort she answered Elijah in a normal tone. "As surely as the Lord your God lives, I don't have any bread—only a handful of flour in a jar and a little oil in a jug. I am gathering a few sticks so that I can make a fire. Then with my bit of flour and few drops of oil I will make a final meal for my son and myself. After that, starvation will come, and we will die."

In gentle tones he answered her. "Don't be afraid. Go home and do as you have said. But first make a small cake for me. Then prepare something for yourself and your son." He paused. As he spoke, mixed feelings had flitted across the woman's face like clouds across a windswept sky. Shock, disbelief, wonder, curiosity, despair, and a flicker of hope chased each other.

With his next words he meant to fan that flicker into a flame. "If you do this," he spoke slowly and deliberately, "Yahweh, the

God of Israel, promises that the jar of flour will not be used up and the jug of oil will not run dry. The Lord will keep His word spoken by His prophet, Elijah!"

The hope flared. The widow's eyes lit with the fire of belief. "Come!" she called, and, nearly running, she led Elijah to her small, two-story stone house. In the kitchen area behind the house she knelt and dropped her few sticks and twigs. Then with her small, brown hands she worked to build the fire.

Elijah watched, a smile in his eyes, as she leaned toward the sticks. Holding her head covering back with one hand, she blew softly and steadily on a smoldering bit of grass until a small yellow flame leaped at the twigs. She blew again, and the flame leaped higher. This time it caught the underside of the sticks. Sudden fire glowed red, yellow, and blue as it crackled up through the mesh of twigs.

Just then a hollow-cheeked boy with thin legs and arms burst into the kitchen area. "Mother! Do we have bread?" he asked.

His mother never slowed in her movements or hesitated in her answer. "Yes, Paddi, we will have bread. But first we will make a barley cake for this man. He is a prophet of Yahweh." For the first time the boy noticed Elijah standing quietly in the shadows.

Paddi watched with hungry, bitter eyes as his mother poured out their last bit of barley meal, mixed it with a little water, patted it into a flat cake, then placed it on the bread sheet over the fire. His mouth watered as she poured their very last glistening drops of oil over the cake. He heard the sizzle and smelled the good smell of the browning barley bread. Then he turned away, tears stinging his eyes, as his mother removed it from the fire and offered it, hot and golden, to the strange man.

Elijah ate slowly, his eyes on the boy and his mother. Turning to the widow, he asked, "What is your name?"

"I'm called Kamzel," she answered.

A twinkle lit Elijah's eyes. "Well, then, Kamzel, why don't you make cakes for yourself and your son now?"

Paddi felt as if he might explode. What kind of mean trick was this man playing, telling his mother to make a meal when he had seen her use every bit of food she had to make bread for him? But he watched with wide, disbelieving eyes as his mother picked up the empty flour jar and tipped it up. To his astonishment, barley meal poured from the jar. She lifted the empty oil jug, tilted it, and poured out enough oil to cook the cakes. The boy rubbed his eyes. How could such a thing happen?

"Your God's promise is true!" his mother said, staring at the Israelite.

Never before had food tasted so good. Paddi smiled as he chewed, his eyes shining. He didn't understand what had taken place. But he knew it must have something to do with this man, Elijah, who wore the clothing of a prophet.

Tears ran down Kamzel's face—tears of gratitude and happiness. "How can I ever thank you?" she asked again and again. "And how can I ever thank your God, Yahweh of Israel?

"You must stay with us!" she suddenly declared. "We have a room on the roof—you can reach it by the outside stairs.

And you may stay there as long as you like!"

"Thank you," Elijah replied.

Elijah kept busy at the widow's home. He mended broken stools, helped Paddi with his chores, and all the time he told about his wonderful, miracle-working God. And at every meal the little family saw God perform a miracle, as barley meal and oil poured out of the containers that never ran empty. Week after week, month after month, God worked His miracle for this widow and her son. Just as God had said, the flour was never used up, and the oil did not run dry. Paddi spent his days following Elijah wherever he went. If Elijah walked about the town, the boy went too. When Elijah talked, Paddi listened. As Elijah stretched and yawned, the child copied him, using the same loose-jointed motions. He even begged his mother to make him a leather loincloth and a camel's hair robe so that he could dress as a prophet like Elijah.

Kamzel smiled at her son's hero worship. And Elijah grew to love Paddi, frequently keeping the boy spellbound with stories of his daring and strange exploits as a prophet.

But one day Paddi did not hurry to greet Elijah when he came down the steps on the outside of the house. Instead the prophet found Kamzel bending over her son, laying a damp cloth across his forehead. A quick glance at his flushed face told Elijah that the child was burning with fever.

For hours Paddi lay on his mat, tossing, moaning, his fever raging out of control. His breath came in weak gasps. Then it seemed that he simply grew too tired to breathe anymore. And he stopped.

Kamzel stared at her son, so alive the day before, now still and lifeless. A sob tore at her throat, and she turned with anguished eyes upon Elijah. "Why did this happen?" she cried. "It must be because your God has seen some sin of mine and is punishing me!" And she threw herself on the floor and wept with all the grief of a mother's broken heart.

Elijah bowed his own head in grief, but said nothing. He did know, however, that God was not punishing this brave widow who had shown such faith in Him. Hadn't God sent him here to bring a blessing to her? Perhaps He wanted to do more for her than provide food each day. Perhaps . . .

With a sudden motion Elijah asked for the child, scooped Paddi up in his arms, then carried him outside and up to his own little room. Laying him on his own mat, he looked at him for a moment before stretching himself upon Paddi's body. "O Lord my God! Let this boy's life return to him!" Hands to hands, face to face, he stretched three times upon the lifeless child.

Suddenly the dead child took a deep breath, opened his eyes, and looked straight into Elijah's smiling face.

The prophet's eyes glowed with happiness. "Shall we go downstairs and see your mother?" he asked softly.

Kamzel still lay on the floor, sobbing as if she would never stop. Holding Elijah's hand, Paddi walked over to her and placed his other hand on her shoulder. "Mother! Don't cry!" he pleaded.

The woman froze. As she whirled to face her son her face turned white while her dark eyes blazed with disbelief turned to joy. "Paddi!" she cried, grabbing him in a hug so tight he couldn't wiggle. Then her gaze met Elijah's. And she understood.

She had trusted this man from a foreign country, and even more than most Israelites, she had believed in the power his God had given him. And because she had, the Lord had blessed her.

With shining eyes and a glorious smile she spoke to Elijah. "Now I know that you are indeed a man of God and that the word of the Lord in your mouth is the truth!"

(The activity for the story of Elijah is found on page 18.)

FIND BABY MOSES

In the grid below, cross out all the squares where baby Moses is not, to find where Miriam hid his basket-boat.

The basket occupies 4 squares.
The basket is hidden in the reeds.
It is not within 2 squares of the sunken boat.
It is not east of the snake.
It is not within 3 squares of the crocodile.
It is north of the sunken boat.
It is not in the quicksand.
It is not north of the quicksand.

④

Mascot Mystery

"So what do you think, Grandfather?" Stacey asked, her voice breathless with excitement. The old man's mansion stood bathed in the long, slanted rays of late afternoon sunshine. Frogs living at the river's edge nearby had already begun their evening chorus, filling the cool air with chirps and groans.

"A parade, huh?" the man said thoughtfully, adjusting his glasses. "Sounds interesting."

Maria, Jason, and Marlene stepped forward, their faces also showing signs of the creative spark kindled by their afternoon conference at the radio station. "We've got it all planned. There'll be two floats, a brass band. Even the mayor of Valley Springs will be there, riding in the first car. We called him on the phone, and he said that as long as voters would be lining the streets, he'd be there."

Professor Appleby grinned. "He said that, huh?"

"Yup," Maria nodded. "Mr. McDonald, that's Marlene's dad, said he'll help us advertise on the radio, and we can put more posters up around town. I'm sure we could get other kids involved too. School's starting in one week, and most of our friends would rather be thinking about something else."

"Anything else?" Jason moaned.

"Well, what do you want *me* to do?" the old man asked.

"You've gotta talk to the college bigwigs," Stacey announced. "They're all adults, you know."

"So I've heard," the professor responded soberly.

"We thought you'd have a better chance of making them see how wonderful our idea is," Jason asserted. "You used to be a teacher and know how to talk college talk. We just talk kid talk. There's a difference, you know. Marlene said so."

Professor Appleby smiled down at the petite girl with the perfect features and carefully styled hair. "You must be very wise," he said.

Marlene extended her hand. "I've heard a lot about you, Professor Appleby. It's a pleasure to finally meet you face-to-face."

"Likewise," the old man said, taking the dainty palm in his big, work-worn, and wrinkled hand. "Your father does a fine job with his station. I listen to it whenever it rains."

The girl blinked. "Whenever it rains?"

"Sure. When the sun's shining I'm out and about seeing to the museum and my visitors. But when it rains, folks tend to stay at home, so I have a few hours to myself. That's when I tune in. He plays beautiful music. And I especially enjoy listening to that woman who comes on at 4:30 in the afternoon. She reminds me of my sister."

Marlene quickly withdrew her hand and stared up at the old man. "But Professor, that *is* your sister. Maggie B?"

"Well," Professor Appleby laughed, "that explains it."

Stacey grinned. "So, will you talk to the college people for us? Maybe you could set up a meeting and we'd show them what we have in mind." The girl paused, a renewed smile lifting the corners of her mouth as she remembered the portly woman with the almost gray hair and kind eyes who had assisted the professor when he set up the museum in his house. "You could get Miss Baker to help. She teaches in the college's History Department. Remember her?"

She saw her grandfather's eyes soften. "Oh, yes," he said. "Miss Baker. Fine woman. Always wore her hair up in a bun. Made her look like a Turkish princess."

"So, how about it? Will you talk to them?" his granddaughter pressed.

"Miss Baker said I was handsome. Fine woman is she. Smart as a whip, too."

"Will you talk to the college people for us?" Stacey urged, trying to get the old man's mind back on the subject at hand.

"Of course I will," he announced with gusto. "If it's a parade you want, then it's a parade you'll get, or my name isn't Professor . . . Professor . . ."

"Appleby," Stacey whispered.

"Appleby," he said, winking at her.

"Great!" Jason said, jumping into the air and giving Maria

an enthusiastic high-five. "We'll get that wing built before you know it."

The old man lifted his hand. "Hold on there," he said. "Have you picked your mascot yet?"

Jason stopped in midcelebration. "Mascot? What's that?"

Professor Appleby shook his head. "Can't have a parade without one."

Marlene stepped forward. "A mascot is a person, animal, or occasionally an object believed to bring good luck to an enterprise or function. It's an old superstition."

"Never mind all that superstition mumbo jumbo," the man said. "Mascots are fun, if you choose the right one. A parade to raise funds for a museum of antiquity should have a proper mascot representing the time and culture the new establishment will reflect."

"But Grandfather," Stacey breathed, trying to steer the conversation away from what looked like an embarrassing situation. "All the people and animals from those cultures are . . . well . . . dead."

"Whatta ya mean?" Professor Appleby chuckled. "The mascot I've got in mind is very much alive. Maggie B talks about them often. Any parade drawing attention to the past should have a mascot that lived in the past, and lives in the present, too."

"I don't understand," Maria frowned. "What lived in the past and also lives in the present?"

The old man lifted his hand. "Listen to the stories tomorrow afternoon, and you'll understand." He smiled. "Just watch the horizon, and look for foreign treasures."

"Watch the horizon? Look for foreign treasures? Then we'll know what mascot we need to find for the parade?" Marlene shook her head. "Sounds like a riddle."

"Maybe it is, and maybe it isn't," the professor chuckled. "Just listen carefully."

The hours seemed to drag by, as they do when a riddle needs time to be solved. But 4:30 the next afternoon finally arrived. Stacey, Maria, Jason, and Marlene all huddled around the portable radio resting on the Roths' dining-room table. Exactly at the appointed time they heard Mr. McDonald silence the music and announce, "It's time for Maggie B's next adventures. Today's stories are about real, God-sent miracles. I think you'll want to stay tuned.

"Elijah the prophet passed from history, but not before he took the time to teach a young man named Elisha everything he knew about God and miracles. Did Elisha learn his lessons well? Just listen."

Stacey glanced at her companions. "You bet we'll listen," she grinned.

✕ ✕ ✕

Timnah shaded her eyes from the afternoon sun and gazed down at the crowd gathering along the dusty road. "Here comes that kind prophet again," she remarked to her husband. "Every time he passes through town he stops to talk with people about God and help them with their troubles. But he must be tired. I'm going to ask him to eat with us and spend the night!"

And while her husband, Dathan, stood there smiling at his warmhearted wife, she dashed into the road and waited for Elisha to come closer. Now that she had made up her mind to offer him a good meal and a place to stay, she could hardly wait for the prophet to reach her.

Greeting everyone took a lot of time. People poured from their homes to greet him, and he stopped to speak with everyone. No simple "Hello, how are you?" would do. They asked about his family, his health, his work, his travels. In turn he inquired about their health, their children, their crops, their mothers, fathers, aunts, uncles, and cousins. The greetings went on and on, as greetings always did in the land where they lived.

Finally he reached the spot where Timnah waited for him outside her home. Bowing low, she welcomed him to the village of Shunem. Then, with a broad sweep of her arm, she indicated the house that belonged to her and Dathan. Elisha gazed at it appreciatively.

The home spoke of wealth and comfort. Sitting atop a sunny hill at the foot of Mount Carmel, it overlooked the great plain of Esdraelon and the mountains of Galilee. A number of animals—

donkeys, sheep, and goats—wandered here and there, while busy servants bustled about. And this home even boasted a second story, a sure sign of a wealthy owner. From the rooftop the family could look to the far horizon and watch occasional caravans moving slowly over the countryside.

"We would be most honored if you would come into our humble home and eat with us," Timnah offered. Elisha smiled. If she had lived in the king's palace, she still would have called it her "humble home"! But he was pleased with the invitation. He had walked all day long, his feet were tired, and he was as hungry as a goat.

After that first meal with Timnah and Dathan, Elisha often stopped to visit with them. Usually he would spend the night, sleeping in one of the servant's rooms. Timnah felt she could not do enough for him. With every visit he told her new and beautiful things about the God of Israel, and her faith in God grew and grew.

One day after Elisha had left them to visit the schools of the prophets, she suggested to her husband, "Why don't we add a room to our house just for Elisha? I know that he's a holy man of God, and I want to do something special for him. We could build a lovely, walled-in room on our roof." Her eyes began to sparkle as she thought of how she would fix it up. "We'll give him his own bed, a stool, and a lamp. Then whenever he comes, he'll know that he has his very own room in which to stay!"

Dathan, looking into her dancing eyes, could only nod his agreement. But when she hurried off to give instructions to the servants, a worried expression crept over his wrinkled face. His mind wrestled with a thought that had been troubling him for a long time.

Much as he hated to admit it, he was old. He wasn't sick or weak—he could still work and manage his estate. But he was old, nevertheless. And Timnah was not. He would die long before she did, leaving her a widow. Then she would be alone.

He thanked the Lord that he had been able to gain wealth. At least, as a widow, Timnah would never have to worry about poverty. But they had no children. Sadly he shook his head and wondered for the thousandth time why the Lord had not blessed them with children. He knew that his wife had suffered with the shame of being childless. People felt that a woman without a child, especially a son, was cursed by God even though God didn't feel that way at all.

If only we had a son, Dathan thought. *He could run my estate when I'm gone, keep Timnah from being lonely, and . . .* His thoughts broke off, and he smiled a sad little smile. *No sense thinking such things,* he told himself sternly. *The Lord has blessed us in many ways. I'll not wish for the impossible.*

Elisha's eyes shone with pure pleasure when he climbed the stairs from the Shunammite woman's courtyard and entered his own newly finished room on the flat roof. It still smelled of fresh plaster and new wood roof beams. An oil lamp, like a little saucer with a pinched rim, sat on a small bedside table. A perfectly carved stool stood in one corner. From a narrow slit of window he could look down on the courtyard below and the hills beyond. And the bed was like something Elisha had seldom seen before. Rare in this land of mats and bedrolls, it boasted four legs and a headboard, a bed fit for a king.

His heart thudding with gratitude, he turned to Timnah, who stood respectfully in the doorway. "How can I ever thank you? You have gone to all this trouble. Isn't there something that I can do for you?" And he did wonder what, indeed, he might do for this kind couple who apparently lacked nothing. What could he possibly give them that they didn't have already?

But he determined to find something. "Would you like me to speak to the king on your behalf? Since Ahab died, I do have some influence. Or perhaps a word to the commander of the army would gain you some special favor . . ." His voice trailed off, and he felt himself floundering. He could already tell by their faces that such offers held no interest for the woman of Shunem and her husband.

Timnah smiled gently. "We're content just as we are, living happily among our neighbors."

Suddenly Elisha's servant, Gehazi, who had followed him up the stairs, leaned over and whispered into his ear. "This woman has no son, and her husband is old."

Elisha's eyes brightened. He understood immediately. Nothing could mean more to this unselfish woman than a son. After offering a quick, silent prayer to God, he turned to her with a broad smile. "About this time next year," he said, "you will hold a son in your arms."

The color drained from Timnah's cheeks, and her dark eyes burned with an old, familiar hurt. Over the years she had trained herself not even to think of having a baby. It had become clear to her long ago that she would not have children. That realization had caused her the deepest grief. But she had accepted the sad truth and put all hope away, like a jewel that had never belonged to her anyway.

Now here stood this holy man of God, telling her that she would have a son! Her voice cracked and broke. "Don't—don't mislead me! Don't give me false hope. I couldn't bear it."

But Elisha had not misled her. The months flew by. And soon Timnah's sadness turned to joy, for a child grew within her. Dathan beamed and thanked the Lord. And just at the time Elisha had predicted, Timnah gave birth to a baby boy.

"We'll call him Micah," Dathan announced, "because the name means 'Who is like Yahweh?'" Timnah thought it a perfect name for her little boy, since he would not even have been born were it not for their wonderful, miracle-working God. Certainly no one could compare to Yahweh.

Little Micah grew strong and sturdy. His chubby legs followed Timnah wherever she went. At the same time his hands were into everything, tangling yarn, tipping over jugs, pulling the ears of woolly lambs. And his sandaled feet explored the courtyard. Often he would come running into the house with a feather for his mother or a pretty flower he had found pushing its way between the mud bricks of the wall.

Timnah's delight in him knew no bounds. And although she sometimes didn't know whether to laugh or cry at some new mischief he invented, she loved him thoroughly and completely. Dathan smiled to see him growing into such a strong little fellow. And he rejoiced even more when Micah started to follow him into the fields, wanting to "help."

One day at the height of the wheat harvest, when even the early-morning sun beat down with searing heat, Micah tagged along after his father. Up and down the field he trudged, his bare feet skimming the sharp, new stubble where the harvesters' knives had cut the wheat stalks. He did his best to gather the wheat in his arms and tie it into bundles, as he had seen the servants do.

But suddenly he dropped his bundle, fell to the ground, and started to cry. "My head! My head!" he moaned.

In one long stride Dathan reached him and knelt beside him on the ground. The child's face twisted with pain. "Quickly!" Dathan bellowed to the nearest servant. "This boy is sick! Take him to his mother!"

Alarmed and shaken, Timnah gathered Micah into her arms. Rocking him, soothing him, she held him close as the hours passed. But at noon his moaning ceased. His little chest no longer rose and fell, for his breathing had stopped. Micah was dead.

Numb with grief, Timnah told herself, *He can't be dead! He can't be dead! Not my little boy that God gave me!* Then she thought of Elisha, the man of God who had promised this child to her. A plan began to form in her mind. "Dear Lord!" she cried. "You gave me my son, and You can give him back to me!" In her sorrow she kept her mind on God. And even though she felt her heart would break, hope and faith told her to expect a miracle.

✕ ✕ ✕

Stacey looked over at her friends, mouth open in surprise. "Did you hear it?"

Maria nodded slowly. "On the horizon? Foreign treasures? I heard."

Jason shook his head. "He's got to be kidding."

"I don't think Professor Appleby was kidding at all," Marlene announced. "That's what we must get for a mascot. It makes perfect sense."

"A camel?" Stacey blurted. "Where are we going to get a camel?"

"I don't know," Marlene sighed. "But it would make our parade extra-special. People would come from miles around just to get a look at one."

Maria scratched her head thoughtfully. "At first I thought maybe a donkey or a goat. But then I understood. The camels were on the distant horizon carrying foreign treasures. We need a camel, all right. Plain and simple."

"There's nothing plain or simple about getting a real live camel to Valley Springs," Stacey countered. "Most folks around here have never seen one at all, me included. Sure, I've looked at pictures in books, but it's not the same as staring one in the eye."

"Hey," Jason interrupted. "The next story is about to begin. Maybe while we listen, we can come up with some ideas."

The group fell into a thoughtful silence as Maggie B's happy voice sounded from the radio speaker.

Timnah stood up, scarcely noticing the weight of Micah's body in her arms. Cradling her dead son as if he were still a baby, she carried him to the door, out into the bright sunlight, into the courtyard. The heat of late summer surged over her, but she paid no more attention to the heat than to the ever-present buzz of flies. Quickly she turned to the stairs on the outside of the house and, still carrying her lifeless child, climbed to the flat rooftop.

Here, on the top of the house, stood the room she and her husband had built for God's prophet, Elisha. With one foot she gently pushed open the door, and entered. Pausing for a moment, she waited for her eyes to adjust to the dimness inside after the bright sunlight outside. The room lay as Elisha had left it, neat and peaceful.

Taking a deep breath, she rapidly crossed the floor to the prophet's bed. Then carefully, tenderly, she placed Micah's body upon it. Tears wanted to run down her cheeks, and her throat ached with the effort to keep from crying. But brushing away her tears with a swipe of her hand, she glanced one last time on Micah's still little body, then left the room, closing the door behind her.

She thought for a moment. *Should I send one of my maids for my husband? No. It's best not to involve too many people in this. I'll go myself to ask Dathan for one of his servants and a donkey.*

Dathan frowned when he saw Timnah approaching. Unlike women whose husbands were not wealthy, his wife did not have to work in the fields. She almost never set foot in the wheatfields, picking her way through the grain and stubble, with all the servants staring, as they were now. *What can she want?* he wondered.

But she gave him little time to wonder. "Please give me one of the servants—with a donkey—so I can quickly go to the man of God, and quickly return!" She waited breathlessly for his answer.

Dathan felt uneasy as he noticed the strained look on her face, the catch in her voice, and the urgency of her manner. "You want to go see Elisha? Why? It's not a new moon or a Sabbath, not the usual time for seeking out a prophet. What's the matter?"

Timnah, however, had determined to keep her sad secret. If she told Dathan, he would be heartbroken. His first move would be to call in professional mourners. And they would fill the air with doleful music and sounds of crying. Soon everyone would know her son had died. But Timnah had a plan based on trust in Elisha's divine power from the God of Israel. And she dared not reveal it, not even to her husband.

So holding her head high and not allowing even one tear to dampen her eyes, she answered calmly, "Everything's all right." And she believed it. Elisha had promised her a son, and Micah was that son. The prophet would somehow summon God's power to bring him back again. She felt sure of it—even as the cold fact of death gripped her with sorrow.

And Dathan, gazing into her honest eyes, agreed to her request, even though he did not understand it. "Of course. Take Darda with you. You'll find him a most reliable servant. Tell him to take the fastest donkey for your trip." With a grateful look at her husband, Timnah turned and ran.

Not waiting for the servant to help her, she threw a thick blanket over her donkey's back and leaped to its back. "Hurry, Darda, hurry!" she urged the servant. "Lead the way to Mount Carmel, where the prophet Elisha stays. Make the donkey go as fast as she can, and don't even turn around unless I tell you. Hurry!"

Darda did as he was told, prodding the animal to clip-clop over the stony road faster than it had ever moved before. Jouncing along through the dust, Timnah clung to the donkey's mane with both hands, while she held her headcloth in her teeth to keep it from blowing away. And while her eyes saw rolling hills and fertile valleys, the dusty road, and Darda's running feet, her heart saw Micah's still form and too, too quiet face.

As they neared Elisha's home, the prophet spotted them in the distance. *What can be wrong?* he wondered. He knew immediately that Timnah had come to him for help. But what kind of help?

"It's the Shunammite woman!" he exclaimed to Gehazi, his servant. "Go meet her. Run!" he urged. "Ask her, 'Are you all right? Is your husband all right? Is your child all right?'"

The servant ran. And he asked. But Timnah answered calmly, "Everything is all right." The woman had not come to see Elisha's servant. She wanted to see Elisha, the prophet of God and the man whose prayers had given her Micah. Suddenly she slid off her donkey, ran to Elisha, and threw herself at his feet, wrapping her arms around his legs.

Her actions shocked Gehazi. What bad manners! To touch a prophet like this! Full of indignation, he dashed forward to push her away. But Elisha understood. "Leave her alone," he told his servant. "She is in bitter distress, but the Lord has not told me why."

Elisha's kind tone released all Timnah's grief. Hardly knowing what she was saying, she sobbed, "Did I ask you for a son, my lord? Didn't I tell you, 'Don't give me false hope'?"

And then Elisha knew. Micah, the miracle child, the joy and pride of Timnah's life, had died. Turning to Gehazi, he commanded, "Tuck your cloak up into your belt and run! Take my staff in your hand. Don't stop to greet anyone—it takes too long. When you get to the Shunammite's house, go in and lay my staff on the boy's face."

Gehazi grabbed Elisha's staff and raced off.

But Timnah was not satisfied. "I will not leave you!" she exclaimed, still holding Elisha's feet.

Gehazi might arrive at her home with Elisha's staff, a sign that the prophet himself would soon be along. The servant might even try to bring Micah back to life before anyone could discover that the child was dead and start to make funeral plans. But through Elisha's word Micah had come into the world. And only Elisha's presence at her child's deathbed would make Timnah content.

The prophet gave her a comforting smile. "Let's go," he said simply.

As they neared Shunem, Gehazi came out to meet them, a discouraged droop to his shoulders. "I laid your staff on the boy's face, but he made no sound, no response at all," he reported sadly.

Elisha nodded and hurried to Timnah's home. As he stepped into his own room, he could see Micah's small form resting on his bed. *So still!* he thought. *So strangely still. This child is never still except when he's sleeping.* Then he smiled. *And that's what he's doing now—sleeping the sleep of death.*

Slowly Elisha walked up to the bed. He stood gazing down at Micah for a moment, taking in the dark, glossy hair, the soft mouth just made for smiling, the long lashes resting on his rounded cheeks. Wordlessly, in motions like those of Elijah's when he had bent over another dead boy, Elisha gently covered Micah's body with his own.

Gradually his own body heat warmed Micah's cold skin. The prophet got up and paced around the room, silently talking with God. Then he again covered Micah's body with his own, hands to hands, face-to-face.

Then—"Ah-CHOO! ACHOO! ACHOO! ACHOO, ACHOO, ACHOO, Ah-CHOO!" Micah's seven sneezes shook the room. Elisha jumped off the bed, beaming with happiness as the child lay there staring at him.

"Thank You, Lord!" the prophet whispered, scooping Micah up into his arms. Then his voice boomed against the walls of his little room. "Gehazi!" he called. "Take this child down the stairs and give him to his mother."

Gehazi started to call for Timnah. But there was no need. She was there, waiting. Her eyes glowed, feasting on her son. Catching Elisha's glance, she bowed to him in gratitude, tears of joy choking off her words.

But as she took Micah in her arms, no words were needed. She hugged him fiercely, nearly bursting with joy as she felt his warm breath on her neck. Her plan had worked. Her trust in Elisha and his God had been rewarded. And Micah, child of miracles, was alive!

✕ ✕ ✕

"Wow," Maria breathed. "That was exciting. Imagine what it would be like to be dead, then alive again." She looked about at the others. "Hey, didn't anyone else hear the story?"

"We heard, we heard," Stacey called. "But before the next one begins, we've got to do some heavy thinking."

"Oh, yeah," Maria sighed. "The camel."

"I know," Jason chimed in. "We can take a horse and dress it up like a camel. Maybe no one would notice."

Stacey rolled her eyes. "Puh-leze. We might fool a bunch of toddlers. But not the whole town. I don't think so. It's got to be a real camel, and that's all there is to it."

"You're right," Marlene agreed. "But"—she wrinkled her pink turned-up nose—"aren't they kinda messy?"

"How do I know?" Stacey asked, throwing up her hands. "I've never had a camel over for supper."

"Quiet, you guys," Jason interjected. "The next story is beginning."

Stacey shook her head. They had to come up with an idea fast. It could mean the success or failure of their grand plan. A camel would bring people to town in droves. It would be a terrific addition to their parade. But where could they find one? Where?

She was still trying to come up with an answer as the next adventure began.

✕ ✕ ✕

Wars. Battles. Raids. Peace—brief and fleeting. Then it would start all over again—the quarrels about land and boundaries, power and trade routes. And now it had happened again.

Syria, Israel's northern neighbor, had swept down on Israel in a fierce raid. As the cavalry's rugged little horses trampled the land and war chariots clattered over the ground, the soldiers killed many Israelites or captured them as slaves.

One frightened Israelite girl screamed as a strong Syrian arm suddenly swung her up into the air. Before she could even struggle, Dinah found herself held in a grip of iron while the horse beneath her galloped away toward an unknown land. "Help, help!" she cried, even while she knew no one could hear her and no one would come to her rescue.

Finally her screams died down, and she whimpered into the gathering night, *Oh, Mother, Father, when will I see you again?* At last even her whimpers ceased. And on that long ride toward Syria Dinah's thoughts turned to God. "Help me, Lord," she prayed. "And I'll not forget You in a strange land!"

The raiding party rode northward, across the desert. But at last darkness called their journey to a halt. Other Israelites, captured as slaves, huddled fearfully on the cold ground. They could scarcely comprehend how their lives had changed.

Dinah cried softly into her headcloth. But when a thin, dark man with surprised-looking eyebrows shoved a piece of bread into her hands, she smiled and thanked him. The man looked more surprised than ever, but managed to find her still another piece of bread.

During the next few days Dinah learned that her new home was in Damascus, the largest and most powerful of Syria's city-states. In spite of being homesick and frightened, she enjoyed the

green grass and colorful flowers. "Damascus is an oasis," explained her new friend, the dark man with the surprised eyebrows. And he went on to describe Pharpar and Abana, the wonderful rivers that watered Damascus. He tried to tell her about the gods of Damascus, too, but Dinah shook her head and smiled.

"You should know the God of Israel!" she exclaimed, and told him about the One who created the trees, flowers, and rivers. "He can work miracles!" she declared, and tried to repeat all the stories her parents had taught her about God's wonderful deeds.

But try as she would to be cheerful, she lay awake at night wondering what the future held. Would she become a slave to some mean person who might whip her and treat her badly? Would she ever see home again? Would the Syrians try to make her worship their idols? She could not answer any of these questions, but as she prayed to Yahweh, the Creator God, He comforted her.

One day her new friend, whose name she learned was Malek, took her straight to Naaman, one of the most important men in all Syria. "This girl will make a willing slave," he told the commander in chief of the army. "Let her serve your wife. I'm sure you won't be disappointed."

Shyly Dinah looked up at the Syrian general. Deep creases lined either side of his mouth before losing themselves in a short, gray beard. His stern brown eyes had a way of looking deeply at whatever his gaze rested upon. And now that gaze rested upon her. She felt it measuring her, probing her intelligence, her health, and her character.

She didn't know why, but she tried not to breathe. Something told her to stand perfectly still and to look straight back at General Naaman, even though she felt like running away. The moments passed. Slowly. And just when she felt she could not bear his searching gaze any longer, he smiled.

She let her breath out in one long sigh. And the general laughed. "She'll do," he decided, nodding in Malek's direction. Then he raised his voice and called, "Basma! Come see what I have here for you!"

The largest woman Dinah had ever seen sailed into the room. Her black, glossy hair was piled on top of her head. Gold ornaments glittered from her throat and wrists. Dinah had never before seen anyone so fancy. Suddenly she felt plain and awkward. And even though she had been able to return the general's stern, steady gaze, her lashes dropped when she felt Basma's eyes upon her.

But a silvery laugh, gentle as rain, startled her. And she looked up into Basma's warm, dark eyes. "Don't be frightened, child," Naaman's wife murmured. "You'll find me a fair mistress. And you look as if you would learn quickly."

Dinah did learn quickly. She helped her mistress in all sorts of ways, running errands, dusting the trinkets and furniture in her big, beautiful home, taking care of all her fancy clothes, combing her mistress's long, black hair. And as she worked, Dinah gradually began to talk about her home, her parents, and the God of Israel. Basma listened, amazed at the stories told her by this young slave girl.

Dinah saw little of Naaman. A busy man, he was away more than he was at home. But every time he breezed into Damascus, people around him stood straighter, walked faster, worked harder, and finally breathed easier when he left. One day, however, as Dinah polished some silver goblets, Naaman came in, threw himself down on a rug, and stared into space.

Basma hurried to his side. "What's wrong?" she asked, her voice full of concern. Without a word Naaman held out his hand. His wife's eyes widened in alarm. Rough, thick patches of reddened skin covered his fingers and crept up his forearm.

Leprosy! The word hung between them, unspoken, but somehow echoing through the room. The Syrians, Israelites, and surrounding nations knew little about skin diseases. But they did know that most of them never got better. The diseases spread. Sometimes they itched, driving the person almost mad. Other types ate away at the flesh. Some simply bleached all the color from the skin, leaving the man, woman, or child with ghostly white patches where healthy skin had once been. Whatever the type of skin ailment, they called it leprosy. And they dreaded this disease, knowing it could not be cured.

Dinah couldn't help staring at her master as he sat on the rug, gazing at his wife with something close to panic in his stern, proud face. *Oh, poor General Naaman!* Dinah thought. But then she had an idea.

As soon as she could speak privately to her mistress, she poured out her suggestion. "General Naaman should go to Israel! Don't you remember my telling you about the prophet Elisha? In the name of our God he has done all sorts of marvelous things. He has even raised the dead. Surely he could cure my master's leprosy."

Cure leprosy? The thought was breathtaking. Basma stared at Dinah. This young girl, a slave from a small kingdom that worshiped a strange God . . . should she take her seriously? All those stories about God's miracles and His prophet's amazing works . . . could they be true? Dinah's eyes, sparkling with excitement, bored into her own.

In a split second she decided. "Naaman!" she called, rushing from the room to find him. And full of hope, she told him of Dinah's idea.

Naaman scowled. The God of Israel? The wild story of a slave girl? A prophet who raised the dead? He shook his head.

"Oh, please!" Basma begged. "What do you have to lose? There is no hope for you here!" And she repeated everything she could remember about Israel's God, everything Dinah had told her.

Slowly Naaman felt himself beginning to believe. "I'll do it!" he decided at last.

But he couldn't just march into Israel, demand to see the prophet, and ask for healing. No, certain procedures had to be followed. Impatient to be on his way once he had made up his mind, he asked his king to write to the king of Israel, requesting permission for a leper to enter and obtain healing. The letter did not mention that Namaan was coming to see Elisha. Naaman delivered the letter himself and brought gold, silver, and 10 new sets of clothes as a present for Elisha.

King Joram of Israel flushed as he read the letter from the king of Syria. "Heal a leper?" he shouted. "Everyone knows it's impossible to heal a leper! Does this king think I'm God? I know what he's doing—he's trying to find an excuse to start another war!" And to show just how upset he was, he ripped his clothes.

But before long Elisha heard of the letter from Syria and how King Joram had torn his clothes. *If only our king would trust God, he wouldn't have ripped his clothes in despair,* the prophet thought sadly.

Summoning a servant, Elisha said, "Run quickly to the king and deliver a message for me!"

King Joram listened, relief and resentment playing tag across his face, as a scribe repeated Elisha's message. "Why have you torn your robes? Have the leper come to me, and he will know that there is a prophet in Israel!" And still fearful and nervous, Israel's king sent for Naaman.

Naaman rode in his elegant chariot. His servants, mounted on horses, trotted on ahead of him. Soon he would arrive at the prophet's house.

He could picture it all now. The prophet, of course, would be honored to have such an important man from Syria come to visit him. No doubt he would come out of his house, bowing and offering a rich meal. After that, he would probably wave his hand over Naaman's diseased arm, speak some magic words, and he would be healed. The Syrian general could hardly wait.

A dusty, stony path led past a lemon tree and grape arbor up to the prophet's house. *Almost there! Almost there!* Naaman thought. Then he could see the house, a small, simple home of mud bricks. The door swung open. And out came—not Elisha, but his servant! With a short, polite bow, Gehazi gave Naaman a message. "The prophet Elisha says to go to the Jordan River. Dip yourself in it seven times, and you will be healed."

Stunned and insulted, Naaman stared furiously at Gehazi. "Drive off!" he shouted to his driver. And his chariot clattered back down the stony path while Naaman muttered under his breath. "Imagine! He didn't even come out to greet me. And he tells me to wash in the Jordan—that muddy stream they call a river. If I wanted to wash in a river, I'd have stayed at home and washed in the clear waters of Abana or Pharpar." But beneath his anger and hurt pride swelled a great sadness and an overwhelming disappointment.

Finally his chariot slowed at the ford of the Jordan, and his servants rode up to him. "Why not consider doing what the prophet asked?" they suggested. "Here we are at the Jordan River. It will never be easier, and you've come all this way."

Naaman tried to think. If Elisha had asked him to do some great thing in order for his leprosy to be cured, he would have done it. He had expected something grand and complicated, but instead the prophet had given him a simple command.

Standing on the bank of the Jordan, Naaman gazed at the muddy water. *How could this river cure his leprosy?* he wondered. But suddenly he remembered the face of the young Israelite slave girl. Her brown eyes were as honest as a child's could be. And they had shone when she spoke of her God and his prophet Elisha.

The memory of those brown eyes gave him courage. And the thought of her faith in God gave him trust in Elisha's directions. "Well, why not?" he muttered, and, throwing off his clothes, he slid down the muddy bank. The cool water closed around his ankles. The mud squished between his toes. But he waded in until the water came up to his waist at the deepest part of the river. Then slowly he bent his knees, feeling the water creep up his chest, to his neck, his chin.

He stood up, glancing eagerly at his hands and arms. No change. The skin was as red, as rough, as thick and ugly as before. But he dipped again. No change. Again he dipped. Again and again and again. Still no change. His servants had been counting each time he sank beneath the water's surface. "One more time!" they shouted. "Just one more time!"

Naaman's face was pale. His lips pressed together in a straight, tight line. He felt his hands trembling. The prophet had said to dip seven times. Already he had dipped six. *O God of Israel!* he cried silently. *If You are there, heal me!*

Again he lowered his body beneath the Jordan's surface. Again he arose. Slowly, almost fearfully, he looked at his skin.

"IT'S HEALED! IT'S HEALED!" he shouted, running, splashing toward the bank. "Look!"

The servants crowded around. They could find no trace of the leprosy, not one rough patch, not one reddened area. Almost reverently his servants touched his skin. It was as smooth and new as a baby's.

Overjoyed, Naaman made his way back to Elisha's house. And this time Elisha stood there waiting for him. "Thank you! Thank you!" Naaman babbled. "Now I understand that there is no God in all the world except in Israel. Here—take these gifts I brought for you." And the servants spread out Naaman's riches before Elisha's astonished eyes.

But the prophet shook his head. "I want no payment," he assured the general. "As surely as my God lives, I will accept nothing. His gifts are free, and it is my privilege to deliver them."

Impressed by Elisha's response in such contrast to many greedy prophets he had seen, Naaman at last turned back toward Syria. But his mind and heart were full of God. He kept stroking his skin, feeling that his own arm was almost holy, for God had touched it.

And on that long journey homeward, he remembered Dinah. What if she had pouted and sulked and kept her mouth closed, fearing to speak of her God in a foreign land? What if she had determined not to help anyone who had taken her away from her home and into slavery?

But she had told all who would listen about the God in Israel. *That girl deserves a reward,* Naaman thought as his chariot bumped and clattered over the rough road. *Perhaps someday I'll give her freedom to her. Perhaps . . .*

But free or not, there was no happier child anywhere than Dinah, the slave girl who had brought healing to her master and a knowledge of God to the land of Syria.

✗ ✗ ✗

"I've got it!" Marlene shouted as the story ended. Her thoughts had been more on their problem than the story. Then, getting a better hold on her emotions, she lifted her chin and smiled shyly. "I mean, I think I have a solution to our dilemma."

"Never mind that," Jason retorted. "Just tell us where we can get our hands on a camel."

Marlene glanced at him, then at Maria and Stacey. "Just look at the pole."

"What?" Stacey gasped.

"The telephone pole in the town square. There's our answer."

Maria sighed. "I think our friend just lost what few marbles she had in her head."

Stacey leaned forward. "Quit talking in riddles, Marlene. You sound like my grandfather."

"But it's all so simple," the girl chuckled. "It's right there on the pole."

"Will you quit with the poles already!" Jason asserted.

"Come. I'll show you," Marlene said, rising.

The others followed her out the door and began walking toward town. Whatever their companion had in mind, it had better be good. If this was a wild goose—or in this case, wild *camel* —chase, there'd be some unhappy parade planners to deal with.

BEFORE AND AFTER

Fill in the letters to describe a character from the story before and after he met God.

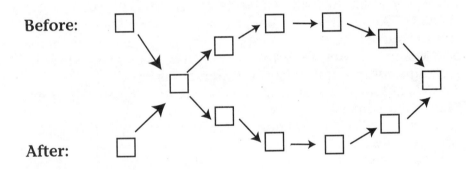

Before:

After:

Letter Bank: A E L L O Y H P R S T H

⑤
Amazing, Stupendous

There. What'd I tell you? The answer's sitting right up on the telephone pole." Marlene pointed with her carefully manicured index finger and grinned broadly.

The children's eyes opened wider and wider as they read the notice printed in bold, red letters. "COME ONE, COME ALL, TO THE TWELFTH ANNUAL BARCLEY BROTHERS CIRCUS. WITNESS AMAZING FEATS OF DARING, EXPERIENCE SPINE-TINGLING ANIMAL ACTS, AND ENCOUNTER FANTASTIC, STUPENDOUS EVENTS NEVER BEFORE GLIMPSED IN THIS PART OF THE WORLD." And right above the picture of a roaring lion, right beside the photo of a man being shot from a cannon, was the image of a woman waving from the back of a very big, very strange-looking creature with a gigantic hump on its back.

"Well, knock me down," Jason gasped. "Marlene's right. There's our camel!"

Stacey studied the announcement thoughtfully. "Yup. That's what it is, all right."

"And they're going to be in Andersonville for the next two weeks!" Maria stated excitedly. "Less than 30 miles away."

"Hey," Jason said, lifting his hand. "Hold on, everybody. Who says the circus people will let us borrow their camel for our parade?"

Stacey glanced at Marlene, a smile playing at the corners of her mouth. "We won't have to borrow it," she said slowly, her eyes returning to the poster. "They'll bring it over gladly, if we can give them a good enough reason to."

Marlene nodded reflectively. "And not only that, they just might bring along that lion and a few other amazing, stupendous, spine-tingling creatures in the bargain."

"Have you two gone bonkers?" Maria breathed. "Valley Springs is a tiny town. We have only one stoplight, and it just blinks."

"Oh," Stacey said, shaking her head, "we have much more than that." She looked at her companions. "Don't we?"

A sudden grin creased Maria's face. "I get it."

"Get what?" Jason asked, scratching his head.

Marlene walked over and placed her hand on the boy's shoulder. "Jason, Jason, Jason," she sighed.

"What, what, what?" he responded.

The girl smiled. "We have *people*—people with cash to spend."

Jason's frown relaxed. "Ohhhh. People who might go to Andersonville and attend the circus if they saw a real live lion—or, might we suggest, a *camel*—right here in Valley Springs."

Marlene nodded. "You're such a smart boy."

He blushed. "I do my best."

Stacey dashed down the sidewalk. "I'm going to check with my mom right now," she called over her shoulder. "I'll call you guys tonight as soon as I know anything. Stay by your phones!"

"We will," the others called after the quickly disappearing girl.

The next afternoon found Stacey, Maria, Jason, and Marlene sitting nose-to-window in Mrs. Roth's station wagon as it rumbled down the country road leading to Andersonville. They had made arrangements to meet with the manager of the Barcley Brothers Circus between shows, when the children would state their case. They'd been rehearsing what they were going to say all morning.

As the countryside whipped by, Stacey glanced at the clock mounted in the automobile's dash. A smile spread across her young face. "Anybody in the mood for a little Maggie B?" she asked.

Heads nodded with enthusiasm. Reaching down, Stacey switched on the radio just as Marlene's dad introduced the first story for the afternoon. She sighed. Seemed Maggie B could be part of their lives even while racing to an appointment with a camel.

"Good afternoon, friends," Mr. McDonald was saying. "Today's stories center on two Old Testament Joes—Joash and Josiah. Before we begin, I want to send a special greeting to four of our young listeners—Stacey, Maria, Jason, and Marlene.

They're on their way to an important meeting you'll be hearing a lot about in the days to come. Good luck, guys!"

The children grinned from ear to ear.

"But now, let's sit back and listen as Maggie B introduces us to 'a wicked grandma and the boy king.'"

✗ ✗ ✗

"Kill them all!" Athaliah, daughter of Ahab and Jezebel, screamed at her soldiers.

The soldiers stared back at her, scarcely believing their ears. Was she out of her mind, or could she really be this cruel? The queen of Judah had just ordered the murder of her own grand-children.

Athaliah was the widow of King Jehoram, a descendant of David. She had not been queen for long. Jehu of Israel had killed her son, King Ahaziah, while the Judean king was on a visit to the northern kingdom. All her relatives there, including her mother, Jezebel, had also perished at Jehu's hands. And Athaliah, greedy for power, had seized the throne of Judah. Now she was deter-mined that no one would take it away from her.

I'll not have any of my son's descendants, who are also descen-dants of David, challenging me for the throne! she promised herself. And with an evil glint in her eye, she again screamed at the sol-diers. "Go! What are you waiting for? Obey my command!"

But God was watching over Judah. In spite of its wicked kings, and now a wicked queen, He still loved His people. And if they must have royal rulers, He would see to it that they were de-scended from David, not Ahab and Jezebel. So while the soldiers carried out Athaliah's evil scheme, God worked out His own plan.

"Quick! Give him to me!" whispered Jehosheba, wife of the high priest, Jehoiada. And someone thrust into her arms a plump baby boy, his dark eyes wide and trusting. "*This* child will not be killed!" she vowed. And holding her little nephew close, she dashed into the Temple grounds, out of sight of the ap-proaching soldiers.

Once inside, she breathed easier. She was in familiar sur-roundings. No one would ever think to look for one of Athaliah's grandchildren here, she reasoned. No, hidden away in the buildings surrounding the Temple, little Joash, a royal heir, a descendant of David, could grow and play with the children of other priests. And if people should see him, they would never suspect that this child was not one of them.

Jehosheba knew she was taking a chance. If Athaliah ever discovered what she had done, the queen would surely have her killed. But Jehosheba felt certain that she was doing what God wanted her to do, and that belief gave her courage. "Now," she whispered to little Joash, "I'll have to find someone who can take care of you." And she did. A young woman who loved God agreed to nurse Joash and raise him just as if he were her own little boy. And this young woman made up her mind that she would teach little Joash to love God.

When he grew old enough to understand, she told him the story of how Solomon had built the Temple and the cluster of buildings around it that the child lived in. She described how splendid and grand it had been before Judah's enemies had raided it, stealing and damaging God's holy property. The sons of Athaliah had done their part, too, stealing its gold and silver to use in the worship of Baal. Besides all this, the Temple was now 200 years old, and ceilings had caved in and big chunks of plaster had fallen off. Such decay and disrepair made Joash sad. He determined that if he ever had a chance to make the Temple beautiful again, he would do it.

The years passed. Two, three, four. . . . Joash lived a strange life behind the limestone walls. His bedroom, safe inside the Temple compound, was in a kind of dormitory where young priests slept. Children of other priests were his only playmates. His foster mother daily taught him all about the history of his people and of the God who cared for them. And while his aunt Jehosheba visited him frequently, and his uncle, the high priest, kept a kindly eye on him, he was never allowed outside the Temple court. The palace where Queen Athaliah lived was right next to the Temple. It was too risky for the child to leave the safety of the Temple.

Then one day all that changed. The very air seemed to pulse with excitement. A plan was under way. The boy in the Temple found himself at the center of a great political plot to overthrow the evil queen. Those loyal to the house of David determined to place Joash on the throne.

For years Uncle Jehoiada had waited for the right time to make his nephew king of Judah. And he had every detail worked out perfectly. At the beginning of the Sabbath, he decided, when all five platoons of soldiers who guarded the palace would be changing places, he would make his move.

But first he had to make absolutely sure that the soldiers he planned to use were completely loyal to him. "We vow our loyalty!" they delcared. Satisfied, Jehoiada led them to the Temple. And there, to their surprise, he showed them a little boy.

Just 7 years old, Joash stared up at the strange men. Who were all these soldiers? Where had they come from, and what did they want with him?

Curious, the soldiers looked at the high priest. Jehoiada's eyes flashed with excitement. The moment had come for which he had waited so long. "This," he exclaimed, with an arm around his nephew's shoulders, "is the rightful king of Judah! He is a son of Ahaziah, and we have hid him here in the Temple ever since the day Athaliah commanded that her grandchildren be killed!

"But today is the day we will take the throne away from her and give it to the house of David's rightful heir!" And at a nod from the high priest, other priests came forward carrying swords and shields. Joash's eyes opened wide. He had seen the weapons before. Kept in the Temple storage rooms for many years, they had once belonged to King David's army. Silently each soldier picked out his weapons. Then a third of the armed men hurried to Joash's side, ready to protect the child who was the rightful heir to the throne.

At a signal from Jehoiada, the others hastened toward the palace. In the midst of the planned confusion—the changing of the guard, when all Athaliah's soldiers swarmed here and there—Jehoiada's soldiers stationed themselves at each entrance to the palace. And just that quickly, Jehoiada's troops took control of the kingdom.

A grim smile on his face, the high priest hurried back to the Temple building in which the soldiers still guarded little Joash. "Come with me!" he said. And Joash slipped his hand into the big, warm hand of his uncle.

Silently Jehoiada led Joash out toward the Temple court. The child blinked as he saw all the soldiers who surrounded the court in a kind of semicircle. All eyes were upon him. He had never before seen so many people. The news of what was happening had traveled like a brushfire. And people from Judah crowded around, jostling each other for a glimpse of the boy whom everyone had thought was dead.

Then Jehoiada stepped forward, holding a gleaming crown in both hands. Reverently he placed it on Joash's head, at the same time handing the child a copy of God's law. The high priest's voice rang out: "Now I proclaim you king of Judah, a son of David, and ruler of our land!"

And as Jehoiada's sons, themselves priests, stepped forward to anoint Joash's head with oil, a mighty shout arose from the throats of the people of Judah. Clapping their hands with joy, they roared, "God save the king!"

The shout found its way to the neighboring palace and into the throne room of Athaliah. "What's happening?" she demanded, jumping to her feet. But in that instant she knew. Rage carried her out into the street. "Treason! Treason!" she screamed, tearing at her robes. But Jehoiada's loyal soldiers met her with the sword and with death.

As the years passed under Jehoiada's watchful eyes, Joash learned how to be a faithful servant to God and His people. His wicked grandmother, just like her mother, Jezebel, had encouraged Baal worship in Judah. But Joash destroyed the temple of Baal and its priests.

More than anything else, however, Judah's new king took pleasure in accomplishing something he had planned to do ever since he was a little boy. He put a great big box outside the Temple and invited everyone to drop their offerings into it. "Your offerings," he assured them, "will pay to restore and repair God's Temple."

People grew excited about the idea. And they gave all that they could. Soon the money box was full. As his servants emptied it, Joash's eyes sparkled almost as brightly as the silver bars. Carefully they weighed them—a lot of money, but not quite enough. "Let's fill the box again!" he declared.

And they did. The people gave generously, willingly. And this time Joash had enough money to restore God's house. The little boy whose home had been the Temple complex became the man who made it sound and beautiful once again.

✗ ✗ ✗

Mr. McDonald cued his microphone. "It's amazing what a young person, with God's help, can accomplish," the man announced, his voice broadcasting out over invisible airwaves. "Looks like nothing is impossible for the Lord."

Stacey smiled to herself as she watched the trees whiz by.

"And now," the speaker continued, "we'll meet our second Joe for the afternoon. It's a few years later but, as usual, God's people need help. And as usual, God responds. I hope you enjoy our second miracle story for the day. It's called 'Discovery in the Temple.' Here's Maggie B."

✗ ✗ ✗

Kneeling in front of her son, Jedidah hugged him. Tall for just

8 years old, he gazed at her with dark, somber eyes.

"Don't forget to honor God, as I have taught you," she urged. "When they place that crown upon your head just a few hours from now, you will be the king of Judah. And as king, you will find yourself surrounded by problems. Everyone will look to you to make wise decisions. You will have people to help you make those decisions, offering all kinds of advice, but some will offer good advice, some bad."

Her voice trailed off as she studied his solemn face. *So much responsibility for a little boy!* she thought. But she had taught Josiah to love God. Now she would have to trust that he would remember the things she had taught him. Suddenly Josiah smiled, bringing dancing lights to the dark depths of his eyes. "Don't worry, Mother," he answered. "I will do what God wants me to do."

And Josiah kept his word. The great-grandson of Hezekiah found that serving God made him happy. The soft glow of the Temple lamps, the murmur of prayers, the smell of incense as it wafted upward toward God, filled him with delight. Every day he talked with God. He told Him his worries and his troubles, things that brought him pleasure and things that made him sad.

And Josiah found plenty to make him sad. Everywhere he went throughout the land of Judah he saw people worshiping idols. Stone altars stood upon scores of hills. And upon those altars, many of them built for the worship of Yahweh, people offered sacrifices to other gods. Josiah's eyes grew big and serious as he watched God's people behave just like those who worshiped the gods of the people of the nations around them.

But Josiah was still a little boy. He thought and he prayed. And he worried. Sometimes he wished he weren't even king. After all, how could he, just one child, stand up to wicked grown-ups, false prophets, evil priests, and corrupt advisers?

But God did not leave Josiah to face his troubles all alone. A few people still served the Lord. One, a woman named Huldah, was a prophet. And she encouraged Josiah to stay true to God. Still other prophets, including Jeremiah and Habakkuk, warned Judah to repent.

The years flew by. Josiah's legs grew longer still. The little boy was growing up. Soon after his sixteenth birthday he began to serve God in a stronger way than he ever had before. And he decided all over again to do whatever God wanted. But with each passing season, he grew more restless. Finally the time came when he could no longer be satisfied simply to pray and think. He had to act.

People stared as he suddenly began to utter crisp commands. "Go up to the high places and throw down the altars of Baal! Break up the altars of incense! Smash the Asherah poles. Grind to powder the idols and the images!" But he not only gave commands, he led the way. Standing atop one high hill after another, he pushed with all his might until the stones of pagan altars toppled over and rolled down the hillside.

The people, however, did not appreciate having their favorite altars and idols destroyed. They had gone so far in their rebellion against God that they did not respect Him, His prophets, or their own king. Loving messages and miracles had not brought them back to God. Nor had warnings and punishment. God's love and patience had not changed them. They respected only one thing—authority backed by force.

And so Josiah uttered one more command. "Put to death the priests who worship idols. Scatter their bones over the broken altars, and burn them." Yet even this drastic action did not turn everyone away from idol worship. Year after year Josiah tried his best to wipe the evil of idolatry from the land.

Soon Josiah turned his attention toward God's Temple. Glorious in the time of Solomon, it had survived looting, neglect, and the ravages of idol worship within its own walls. Even now, images and idols littered its sacred courts and chambers. Dirt and rubble clogged its passageways. The walls stood crumbling, and curtains hung in tatters. The gleaming floor lay hidden beneath layers of dust and filth.

One day, as Josiah walked through the Temple courtyard, his young shoulders slumped with weariness. What could he do to restore God's house to its original glory? Then, eyes flashing with determination, he set to work. Quickly organizing the priests, he gave them instructions. "You take charge of the expenses, Hilkiah," he instructed the high priest. "And you"—he indicated some of the Levites—"oversee the labor."

The work moved forward. Josiah smiled each time one of the hated images sailed through the air to land outside in a rubbish heap. Later, the workers would burn the wooden idols and smash those made of stone. The young king could hardly wait until God's Temple again stood purified and proud, shining in its holiness.

Each day the rubbish heap grew bigger and the Temple became cleaner. Then one day as Hilkiah directed the removal of gold and silver from the Temple treasury, he happened to poke into a dark corner in a neglected room. And there he spotted an old, beat-up wooden chest. Curious, he lifted the lid. With a sharp intake of breath, he bent over its contents. A stale smell met his nostrils.

Whatever can these things be? he wondered as his eyes fell on some rolled-up leather. *They must be very old.*

He gazed for a long moment at the rolls of tightly coiled leather, covered with dust and grime. Then, cautiously, he lifted them from their resting place. *Scrolls. Old scrolls—hidden here in the Temple. What could be written on them?*

Sinking to the floor, he began to read the faded words, inked onto the leather in neat columns. He read and he read. And when he finally looked up, his eyes were full of tears. He had found the book of the Law, given long ago through Moses. Never before had he seen these words of God written down. He had heard them spoken—had recited them himself. But they had become only something the priests said in the Temple services, not a part of the people's daily life. His people had forgotten so many things!

A ray of sunlight from an opening high up in the wall bathed Shaphan, the royal secretary, as he went from one room to another. "Shaphan!" Hilkiah cried when he saw him. "Come here!" His voice shook with eagerness. "I must show you what I have found."

And now Shaphan read while a look of wonder spread across his sun-creased face. When he had finished, he gathered up the scrolls, holding them as tenderly as a mother holds her infant, and started toward the palace.

Shaphan's heart thudded in his chest while waiting for Josiah to receive him. *The law of Moses!* How long had it lain there? Had some priest hidden it to keep it safe from priests of other gods or from invading pagan soldiers? Had someone just tossed it into the chest like some piece of rubbish, and then forgotten about it? Could it have been a scroll that the priests had thought too worn to continue to use, and had put into storage?

No one had known, no one had suspected, that such a precious document lay under centuries of dust, easily within reach, but out of sight.

Josiah's dark eyes missed nothing as Shaphan stood before him, trembling with excitement. The royal secretary clutched a heavy roll of leather, darkened with dirt and age.

"What is it?" Josiah asked quietly, even while he felt on the verge of some wonderful discovery.

"Hilkiah found this book in the Temple," Shaphan answered softly. "Listen!"

Then he began to read. His voice rose and fell in rhythm with the majesty of the words and the strength of his own feelings. And Josiah listened to the words God had given to Moses so long ago.

"'Remember the covenant I made with you at Sinai—the Ten Commandments,'" the royal secretary chanted. "'Observe them carefully, and other nations will wonder at your wisdom. What other nation has a God who by mighty deeds and an outstretched arm delivered them out of the smelting pot of Egypt?

"'So acknowledge your God. Take His words to heart. Obey His commands. If you do, things will go well for you and your children, and you will live in the land that I have given you for all time.

"'But watch yourselves carefully. Don't fall into idolatry. And when you look up to the sky and see the sun, the moon, and the stars—all the heavenly array—do not be charmed into worshiping them.

"'After you have had children and grandchildren and have lived in the land I have given you for a long time—if you then become corrupt and make any kind of idol, you will quickly perish from the land. The Lord will scatter you among the peoples, and only a few of you will survive among the nations.

"'But even there, if you seek the Lord your God, you will discover Him. If you search for Him with all your heart and soul, you will find Him. Then, when you have returned to the Lord your God with loving obedience, He will not abandon you, for

He is merciful, and will keep the covenant He made with your forefathers.

"'Now hear the words of the law:

"'You shall have no other gods before Me.

"'You shall not make for yourselves an idol in any form, nor bow down and worship one.

"'You shall not use carelessly the name of the Lord your God.

"'Observe the Sabbath day to keep it holy, doing all your work in six days, but resting on the seventh.

"'Honor your father and your mother.

"'You shall not murder.

"'You shall not commit adultery.

"'You shall not steal.

"'You shall not give false testimony against your neighbor.

"'You shall not covet anything that belongs to your neighbor.'"

Shaphan paused, a lump in his throat. He knew how far God's people had strayed from those commandments. Then he read these words:

"'Hear, O Israel, the words of the Lord. Love the Lord your God with all your heart and with all your soul and with all your strength. These commandments that I give you are to be upon your hearts. Impress them upon your children. Talk about them when you sit at home and when you walk along the road, when you lie down and when you get up. Never forget them. Keep them ever before you.'"

Shaphan stopped. There was more. Much more. But what he had read was clear. Terribly clear. God loved His people. He had begged them to trust Him, follow Him, obey Him. In return He had promised them a land of their own, health and wealth, protection against their enemies, and blessings too numerous to count. But they had not listened.

He looked up to see Josiah gazing at him through pain-filled eyes. With a sudden groan the king clutched his clothes and ripped them at the neck. His sorrow was too deep for words. Only by this action could he express his agony for his people. *Oh, how,* Josiah wondered, *could we have strayed so far from the commands of our loving God?*

When he could finally speak, he summoned some of the most important people in his court, people who served the Lord. Standing silently before the king, they waited for him to make known his wishes.

Josiah cleared his throat, then spoke in a low but urgent tone: "Go to Huldah. Ask her what the Lord has to say about me, about those who are left in Israel, and about the people of Judah, for we have not followed the words written in this book." The men were well acquainted with Huldah the prophet. Always involved with whatever was going on in Jerusalem, she and her husband lived in a small stone house toward the northern extension of the city. Quickly the men left the palace, hiking the familiar hilly streets.

Smiling a warm welcome, Huldah met them in her courtyard. But the smile lasted only a moment, for she knew why they had come. She knew the sins of God's people. And she realized that God, amazingly patient during hundreds of years of rebellion, would finally bring punishment upon them.

Before they had even asked their questions, she answered them.

"Tell this to the man who sent you," she instructed, referring to King Josiah. "This is what the Lord says: 'I am going to bring disaster on this place and its people. All the curses that have been read to the king of Judah will come to pass. Because My people have forsaken Me and burned incense to other gods, My anger will be poured out on this place.

"'But because you humbled yourself before God when you heard what He spoke against this place and this people, and because you tore your robes and wept in My presence, I have heard you,' declares the Lord. 'You, Josiah, will be spared the disaster soon to fall upon this place and those who live here. And you will be buried in peace with your ancestors.'"

Josiah felt that his heart would break when his messenger repeated Huldah's words to him. He loved God's people, wicked though they were. Yet he knew that God was fair. The Lord had tried in every way imaginable to protect His people by His laws. But they had turned away from Him to dance before idols. Without shame they had sprawled naked upon the Temple rooftop as they worshiped the sun, moon, and stars. And they had burned sacrifices to gods of wood and stone upon Yahweh's sacred altars.

But Josiah had remained true to God. When only 8 years old he had trusted God. At 16 he had turned to Him with all his heart. And ever after, he had tried in every way he knew to turn God's people back to Him.

And now at this time of sadness, God's smile comforted him, even as Josiah's loyalty comforted God.

⚔ ⚔ ⚔

The story ended just as Mrs. Roth's car roared past the Welcome to Andersonville sign. Stacey switched off the radio and sat back against the seat, a nervous sigh drifting from her lips.

Mrs. Roth turned and smiled. "You'll do just fine, honey," she said softly. "It's a great plan, especially when I tell them I'll be covering the story in our town newspaper. When they see how many subscribers we've got, I think they'll be impressed."

Her daughter nodded shyly. "What if they say no?"

"Then I'll dress up like a camel and lead the parade down Main Street," Mrs. Roth announced.

Stacey burst out laughing. "Oh, Mom. You'd make a terrible camel. You don't look anything like the one in the poster."

"Makeup," the woman declared. "It's all a matter of makeup."

The children in the back seat added their voices to the laughter echoing from the automobile as it edged its way into the city traffic. A huge billboard over one of the office buildings up ahead cried out its message of guaranteed fun for all at the Barcley Brothers Circus, now playing at the fairgrounds. Right in the middle of the billboard was the image of a camel, standing proud and tall, looking down at the citizens of Andersonville from its lofty perch. Stacey, Maria, Jason, and Marlene weren't sure, but it seemed as if the animal were actually smiling.

BIBLE PEOPLE

```
J  P  I  L  I  H  P  H  B  E  C  O  O  F  J
J  M  B  H  M  L  A  N  L  O  H  J  Z  C  S
E  A  D  U  X  U  K  I  H  A  E  Y  K  C  H
Y  I  Q  L  P  E  J  A  I  H  G  J  T  G  A
E  R  C  D  V  A  I  L  O  G  A  Y  B  U  R
M  I  J  A  H  S  A  S  O  H  K  W  U  V  H
A  M  V  H  O  H  H  U  A  J  E  S  U  S  P
R  A  N  J  T  E  J  B  H  R  J  W  R  B  I
M  A  A  A  B  N  J  O  D  E  J  U  Y  K  H
A  R  M  A  V  H  F  N  C  E  J  J  B  O  S
R  O  A  T  U  Z  A  Q  Z  H  L  Y  B  U  E
E  N  A  R  M  O  S  E  S  L  E  I  H  E  G
K  E  N  F  X  B  B  S  C  I  M  B  S  H  I
R  O  L  X  C  E  J  X  C  X  T  K  E  H  X
O  B  J  Y  L  D  W  J  R  V  Y  J  O  D  A
```

Aaron	Huldah	Miriam
Ahab	Jehosheba	Moses
Amram	Jehu	Naaman
Andrew	Jesus	Philip
Athaliah	Jezebel	Puah
Elijah	Jochebed	Shiphrah
Elisha	Josiah	

6
The Three Visitors

This is WPRL, the hometown voice of Valley Springs." Mr. McDonald shuffled the papers spread across his audio console and smiled at his unseen audience. "As everyone who's been listening to this radio station during the past week knows, today's a very important day for our town. No, it's more than important. It's incredibly, most assuredly, absolutely certainly the most special day Valley Springs has seen for a long, long time."

Stacey reached over and turned down the volume of the battery-operated radio resting on the park bench beside her. "Your dad surely is in good form this afternoon."

Marlene grinned. "Words are his business. At least, that's what he keeps telling me."

The two girls had arrived at the square early to make sure everything was ready for the big parade. Announcements had appeared in the newspaper and over the radio and a hundred and one arrangements finalized, including getting the local volunteer fire department to kick off the parade with their one and only bright-red fire truck. They promised wailing sirens and flashing lights, exactly what a good fund-raiser needed to catch the attention and stir the hearts of the people who'd be lining the street.

Professor Appleby and the community college public relations board had labored day in and day out, making sure all would run smoothly. The parade would be the institution's big chance, a concerted effort to draw attention to the planned Appleby-Brewster Museum of Antiquity wing scheduled for construction on the campus—if enough people promised to support their dream.

They had planned the parade right down to the second. First the fire truck would thunder through the square, loudly announcing the beginning of the parade. The high school marching band, hastily regrouped and thoroughly practiced, would immediately follow.

Town and college officials would arrive aboard shiny antique cars on loan from a local businessman who enjoyed rebuilding automobiles from years past.

The local chapter of 4-H was even now gathering at the staging area behind the discount store. Young people guided carefully groomed sheep, scrubbed and cleaned cows, along with bleating goats through the milling crowd of future farmers and ranchers.

Mrs. Roth and Mr. McDonald would arrive next riding in the radio station manager's brightly decorated truck. "Support the Museum" signs had been fitted to rise high above the vehicle's cargo area, inviting everyone to "be a part of history."

The parade would circle the square three times, then come to a halt by the reviewing stand. Mr. Deardorff, Valley Springs mayor, would climb up to the podium and give a speech. Then Dr. Morrison, president of the community college, would do the same. Professor Appleby had been invited to say a few words after that. Stacey could hardly wait to hear what her grandfather had planned.

Junior Darby and the Home Town Fiddlers, a popular group made up of hardworking members of the community, would entertain with their repertoire of country-Western tunes interspersed with lots of down-to-earth storytelling.

Most of the acts in the parade had performed before in Valley Springs, but never all on the same day. Everyone in town was looking forward to this outpouring of local talent and enthusiasm.

That's why even now, an hour before the parade was scheduled to begin, the streets were already filling with happy faces and reverberating with excited voices as friend greeted friend and neighbor waved at neighbor.

"Where's Jason?" Stacey asked nervously from where she sat on the curb, looking across the teeming avenue at the alleyway leading to the back of the grocery store. "He said he was just going to be a minute."

"Probably got lost in the warehouse," Marlene chuckled. "Let's just say our friend isn't exactly the best at navigation. Remember when he was going to show us his secret cave last Tuesday and we ended up at Mr. Bloomenburg's gas station down by the railroad tracks? If Jason had been on the *Mayflower,* we'd all be living in the South Pacific someplace."

Stacey laughed out loud, her nose turning red, as it usually did when something tickled her funny bone. She glanced over at her companion. "I like you better this way," she said.

"What way?" Marlene asked, tilting her head slightly.

"You know. Like a kid instead of a grown-up. We're almost the same age, yet sometimes I feel you're trying to be 20 or something."

Marlene blushed. "Really?"

"Yup."

The girl studied her highly polished, scuffless running shoes. "That's because I'm the woman of the house."

"What do you mean?"

Marlene glanced down the street at the building housing her father's radio station. "Since Mom died, Dad's had no one to take care of him—you know, clean the house, cook the food, listen to him when he bellyaches about this or that. So I figured I could do all those things. He keeps telling me to be a kid and how I should be out playing in the mud or something. But when he's troubled, or his radio station business isn't doing too well, I know the last thing he needs is some little brat running around the house making noises and bothering him.

"It makes me feel grown-up when I take care of him, even though I know I'm only 10." Marlene smiled at Stacey. "My mom was so . . . so . . . perfect. She was the best. I miss her. It helps when I try to be like her—you know, dress like she did, with everything pressed and clean." The girl sighed. "My dad needs me, and it makes me feel glad when I do stuff for him. He's the best too."

Stacey stared at her companion for a long moment. When she spoke, her words were gentle. "Well, what do you know? I thought you were acting all high and mighty because you were stuck-up or something."

Marlene kicked at a stone. "Until my dad met your mom, I didn't get a chance to play with kids too much. Didn't have time. You don't understand my father. If I wasn't looking after him, he wouldn't know what to do. I remember Mom saying he was pretty pitiful, just like a helpless puppy dog." She paused. "Some men need to be taken care of by a woman. My dad's one of 'em."

Stacey shook her head. "My mom's always telling me not to judge people until I've gotten to know them. Man, I had you pegged all wrong. You're OK, Marlene, in a weird sorta way. I guess you really are 10 going on 20."

Marlene grinned. "I'm glad we're friends. Who knows? Maybe someday we'll be sisters. I'd like that."

"Me too," Stacey nodded. "But I'm no puppy dog. You won't have to look after me."

Just as Marlene was about to respond, a young male voice called from across the street. "It's gone!" The announcement arrived with a hint of desperation. The two girls looked up to see Jason racing toward them, weaving his way around groups of early-bird parade watchers.

"What do you mean?" Stacey called, rising to her feet.

"It's just gone. Mr. Brandon asked me to look after it so he could get some doughnuts. While he was away, I took a break to check out the dumpster—found an old watch that's still ticking—and when I got back, it had vanished into thin air!"

"This is terrible!" Stacey gasped.

"No, this is worse than terrible," Marlene groaned. "Without it the queen of the parade, that's me, has no escort. Royalty isn't supposed to *walk*. It's not proper. And let's not forget, if we don't find it, they'll throw us in jail for sure. Come on!"

The three hurried away, leaving the radio playing quietly on the park bench, Mr. McDonald's voice calling out to the passersby.

"And now, boys and girls, ladies and gentlemen, it's time for our afternoon visit with Maggie B!" the speaker said cheerily. "Looks like we can play three stories before the parade begins. So kick off your shoes, close your eyes, and journey with me to a small town near the Sea of Galilee, where we'll meet a little boy with a very big problem."

☒ ☒ ☒

In the city of Capernaum a black stone house lay wrapped in sadness. Brothers and sisters tiptoed about with long, unhappy faces. The father paced back and forth, hands behind his back, a deep, worried frown wrinkling his forehead. And the mother never left a dark and silent room where little Ehud lay burning with fever.

The servants hurried back and forth with water. Mother constantly bathed Ehud's hot face and thin little body. Finally a door opened, and a doctor bustled into the room. Mother stood aside while Father crouched beside the child and the children gathered around with big, scared eyes.

The doctor felt Ehud's forehead. He lifted the boy's eyelids and peered into his eyes. Then he placed his hands on Ehud's chest, feeling each slow and shaky breath.

Finally he turned to Mother. "Have you given him the medicine I left the last time I came?"

Mother nodded.

"Did you give him water from the mineral spring? Did you mix the herbs exactly as I directed? Did you give him powdered garlic in water?"

With each question Mother nodded, while tears slid down her cheeks.

At last the doctor cleared his throat and, without looking at anyone, said, "I'm sorry. There's nothing more that I can do. Keep him as comfortable as you can. He can't last much longer."

A sob broke from Mother's throat, and Father stumbled from the room, bowed and bent. The children scattered to private corners where they could cry without being seen.

How could this be happening? they all wondered. They remembered when little Ehud had been strong and healthy, teasing and playing, running and jumping. Now for weeks they had watched him grow weaker, thinner, sicker. And no one could make him better.

In the scant shade of the north side of the house Father paced, biting his thumb as he sometimes did when worried about something. And all the while an idea grew in his mind. *What about the Healer, Jesus?* He had heard about His daring deeds at the Temple, and of the scores of people who claimed He had healed them from one ailment or another.

Father had his doubts, of course. The Man was known to come

from simple people in the lowly village of Nazareth. He found it hard to believe He had any supernatural powers. Yet—it was worth a try. At this point he had nothing to lose.

Having made up his mind, he felt better. At least he would be doing *something*, not simply giving up. Hurrying inside to his wife, he explained his plan. He would leave at sunrise the next morning.

I wish Jesus were staying here in Capernaum, he thought. *But He's in Cana now, and it can't be helped. Still—it will take hours of hard walking to reach Him!*

He awoke the next morning while it was still dark. Ehud had lived through the night, his hot, dry skin cooling ever so slightly with the chill of sundown. But he was so weak.

Father stepped into the gray mist of morning. As the summer sun peeped over the eastern hills he could already feel its heat. In a few hours that heat, blending with the damp air from the lake, would wilt every living thing.

"My child!" Father whispered to himself, thinking of Ehud. "Why do you have to suffer so?" Day after day he had watched Ehud's fever climb with the sun—burning the life out of his little body.

Father trudged around the shore of the Sea of Galilee, too busy with his thoughts to notice the beauty of the morning—vapors rising over the still, blue water; hills of lavender ringing the lake like sleeping giants.

All day he walked, then found a place to sleep during the night. The next morning he started on his way again. Finally, panting, he climbed the steep, rough road leading to a little village perched high above the Valley of Gennesaret. Despite his anxiety to reach Jesus quickly, he stumbled into the shade of an open-air marketplace. Wiping the sweat from his forehead, he looked around.

People were staring at him with a mixture of curiosity and suspicion. *My clothes have given me away!* he concluded. And it was true. The common people had immediately spotted the fine weave, rich colors, and fancy designs that proclaimed him a royal official, probably from Herod's court.

Lips curled in barely disguised sneers. *Another Jew who has sold out to the Romans!* he knew the people thought with disgust.

But Father didn't care what the people thought or said about him. His mind was on one thing only—getting to Jesus so that his son might have a chance to live. Feeling a little better after a short rest and a drink of water, he hurried on his way.

The sun beat down as he plodded on again in a cloud of insects. Dust caked his lips, seeped into his mouth and nostrils, while tiny rivers of sweat trickled down his body. But one thought kept him going—Ehud, his son.

About the sixth hour, with the sun almost directly overhead, he reached the hill on whose summit rested the village of Cana. Facing the steep, rocky slope, he took a deep breath and willed his tired legs to climb.

At last—Cana! Hurrying down a dusty trail, he suddenly spotted a horde of small boys jostling one another to peer through the doorway of a house. Father asked them what they were trying to see. "It's Jesus," one child said. "The One who turned water into wine at the wedding. We want to see Him do another miracle." Father's heart thudded with excitement. He had found Him!

Pushing his way into the little house, he elbowed through the crowd until he suddenly came face-to-face with the Healer. A wave of disappointment washed over him.

The Man looked so *ordinary.* A white headcloth, no different from that of any peasant, fell to His shoulders. The rough cut and weave of His clothes marked Him as a poor man. His sandals were worn. He was not especially tall or good-looking and didn't look at all like anyone with special powers.

Still, Father reasoned, *I've come all this way in the hot sun. I'm tired. My feet are bleeding from thorn scratches. I have insect bites all over me—and Ehud lies near death! It would be foolish to go back without even asking Him to heal my son. But if He doesn't, I'll never put my trust in Him again!*

So with the thought of Ehud, burning with fever, uppermost in his mind, Father seized Jesus' sleeve, and asked, "Please, Sir, would You come to Capernaum with me and heal my son?"

Jesus gazed into Father's worried eyes. And He saw in them all the man's love for his son. He even saw little Ehud on his bed, and Mother and the children, silent and teary-eyed.

But He saw something else. He recognized Father's doubts and read his every thought as clearly as if they had been written on a scroll. And Father's thoughts reminded Him of so many other people who would not believe in Him unless they witnessed wonders and miracles.

His memory rested for a moment on the Samaritan woman at the well, and on the other Samaritan people who accepted Him and loved Him without asking for miracles. If only His own people would trust Him like that!

Placing both hands on Father's shoulders, Jesus gazed deeply into his eyes. With a sad little smile He murmured, "Unless you people see signs and wonders, you simply do not want to believe at all!"

Father felt desperate, as if he were standing on the seashore while great waves washed in, tearing the sand from beneath his feet. Forgetting the crowd around him, forgetting his doubts, he cried, "Sir! Come down before my child dies!"

Jesus' eyes filled with pity and boundless love. But He didn't need to go to Capernaum. His power, the wonderful power of God, was already there.

He smiled kindly at Father. "Go on home. Your son will live."

Suddenly the weariness left Father's body. He felt like a boy again. *Ehud would live! Ehud would live!* He knew it. Jesus had said so, and he believed Him. How had he ever thought the Man was ordinary? Why, anyone could see that He was sent from God!

Much later, as Father neared Capernaum, he spotted his servants racing toward him. "Come, Master! Come!" they shouted. "The boy! Little Ehud—his fever has broken!"

To their amazement, their master didn't act at all surprised. Just happy. But he did question them closely about Ehud's recovery. "When, *exactly*, did he get better?" he asked, staring at them intently.

"Why, it was the hottest time of the day, at the seventh hour, that the fever left him," they answered, wondering why that was so important.

They couldn't understand the flash of joy, of unshakable confidence, in Father's eyes. *The seventh hour! The very hour when Jesus had said, "Your son will live!"*

✕ ✕ ✕

Stacey shook her head in frustration. "I don't believe this. I just don't believe this. We've been all over the warehouse and up and down the alleys. Then we checked the old train station and every hiding place within four blocks. It's disappeared. That's the only explanation."

Jason pointed in the direction of the street. "Hey, there's Deputy Steward from the police department. Maybe he's seen it."

Stacey lifted her hand. "Wait. We can't tell him what we're looking for. It's supposed to be a surprise for the whole town. If he finds out, he might blab our secret all over the place."

"You're right," Jason breathed. "We'd better watch what we say."

The three children approached the man standing by the outdoor fruit display in front of the grocery store. "Hey, Deputy," Stacey called, a smile lighting her face.

"Hi, Stacey," the man responded, tapping the brim of his hat with his finger. "And how you doin', Jason and Marlene?"

"Fine," the other two children stated.

Stacey cleared her throat. "Say, Deputy. Have you seen anything strange running around here in the past few minutes?"

"Strange?" the police officer asked.

"Yeah. You know, kinda out of the ordinary."

The man frowned. "What do you mean?"

Stacey looked around, then leaned forward slightly. "We're looking for something that's kinda ugly, has hairy ears, a big nose, and spits a lot. It also makes strange noises from time to time."

Deputy Steward laughed. "You must mean my cousin Rosie. No, I haven't seen her all day."

Stacey blinked. "Well, uh, thanks. We'll be going now."

"Sorry I couldn't help," the police officer said with a snappy salute. "But if I run into Rosie, I'll let her know you're looking for her."

The children smiled weakly. "Great. See ya," they said. With a wave, they disappeared into the crowd.

Across the street a group of youngsters had gathered around a radio perched on the park bench. The kindhearted voice of Mr. McDonald rose above the tumult and commotion.

"Our second adventure reveals another miracle performed long-distance. I know you'll like this one. Here's Maggie B."

✗ ✗ ✗

Leprosy.

In all the land no word produced such dread, such terror and loathing. And anyone unfortunate enough to catch the disease knew he or she was doomed to a living death.

Somehow Yabal had caught it. He remembered the day he had first discovered a small white patch on the back of his hand. Thoughtfully he had rubbed it with the forefinger of his other hand. It felt strange—sort of numb—as though it was dying.

A bolt of fear rammed his innards. *Leprosy?* It couldn't be! Why, surely in a day or so the spot would disappear. He laughed aloud, nervously, shakily. No need to panic.

But the spot didn't disappear. It grew. And others came. He tried his best to hide the telltale patches from everyone. Some looked darker than his normal skin color, some lighter. Eventually the day arrived when his wife noticed the strange splotches on his hands and face.

Horror stared out of her wide, dark eyes. As their little boy toddled into the room, she screamed at Yabal, "Don't touch him!"

With a sob Yabal stumbled from the house, the sound of his wife's crying following him into the street. The time had come. He could no longer avoid it. Yabal would have to show himself to the priests. They would examine him. And if they found he had leprosy, he would be banished. He would join the scores of other lepers as they flitted like sad gray shadows along the outside walls of the city, crying in mournful tones, "Unclean! Unclean!"

The priests took one look at him and shrank back in fear and disgust. "You have leprosy!" they shouted. "Away with you! No unclean thing shall pollute the holiness of Israel!"

The years passed in a miserable blur. His voice grew hoarse from calling "Unclean! Unclean!" Women snatched their children out of his path whenever they heard that fearful warning. Unable to work, he resorted to begging. But as he held out his clawlike hand, people shouted, "Get away from here, you stinking leper!"

Often he heard men explaining to their sons, "God is angry with that man because of his sins. That's why he has leprosy." Always they shrank from him. Their greatest dread was that he might somehow touch them. People even ran from his shadow.

And the disease grew worse. He no longer had any sensation in his feet or his hands, and they were marred with horrible scars from burns and cuts he had never felt. The muscles in his face had grown stiff and numb. The cartilage and bone in his nose had crumbled, so that people he once knew, even his wife, would have had trouble recognizing him. His eyelids would close only with the greatest difficulty, and the bright sun shone mercilessly into his unprotected eyes, slowly burning them blind.

One time he caught a glimpse of his son, now grown tall, in an alleyway near the city wall. "Unclean! Unclean!" Yabal called, his voice and heart breaking. His son glanced his way, not recognizing him, an expression of fear in his eyes. But Yabal saw something else there, too—pity, mixed with the sadness of a little boy who had lost his daddy to leprosy so many years ago.

And Yabal wondered. Had all this really come upon him because he was so bad? Did God hate him that much?

One day as he huddled miserably with a group of other lepers, sharing a thin soup made from other people's garbage, a young fellow, one of the few who still appeared healthy, spoke up. "I heard today about a Man who heals all kinds of diseases. Even leprosy."

Clatter and conversation stopped. Then everyone burst out talking. "Even leprosy? Where is He? What's His name?"

"The last I heard, He was in Capernaum. And His name is Jesus."

The faintest glimmer of hope flickered in Yabal's breast. The more he heard about Jesus, the stronger grew that hope. He made up his mind that he would somehow find Him.

Banned from cities, he limped over rough and twisting mountain roads, dodging into the brush whenever another human approached. Once, as he crouched in the bushes, he heard people talking about Jesus. "He has never turned anyone away!" some-

one said. And Yabal, for the first time since he had developed leprosy, felt like singing.

At last he reached the Sea of Galilee. Crowds of people swarmed the rocky shore, the overflow spreading up the rocky bank onto a narrow strip of grass. Timidly he inched closer. Then he spotted a Man in the center of the crowd. That Man radiated kindness, goodness, love. The people couldn't seem to get enough of Him as they hung on to His every word.

His loving glance included everyone—men, women, and little children. Yabal strained to hear His words but couldn't quite understand them.

He inched closer.

Again he was struck by the pure goodness of the Man. Suddenly doubts overwhelmed him, swallowing him, smothering him. Wouldn't this Man, too, flee in terror from his presence? Wouldn't this good Teacher look with horror on a man everyone said was under the curse of God? *I must be a terrible sinner!* Yabal thought.

But something different was happening. Sick people from the crowds stumbled toward Jesus. The lame, the blind, the paralyzed, all—one way or another—made their way to Him. And in tones of tenderness Jesus pronounced them well. And they were!

Yabal saw a woman who had been so ill she couldn't hold her head up raise her face and her arms toward heaven, praising God. Lame people pranced like children. Blind people laughed and cried as they gazed into the faces of their friends and loved ones, at the beautiful, sparkling lake, or puffy white clouds in a blue sky. Most wonderful of all, they looked into the face of Jesus.

Yabal took courage. Hope drove him forward. Staggering, stumbling, he ran toward the crowd, toward Jesus.

Then the people spotted him. Screams and shrieks of terror filled the air. In a panic the crowd tumbled all over itself as it scrambled madly away in all directions. Some even plunged into the lake.

But one Man did not move. Jesus' eyes shone with love and pity as Yabal headed toward Him. He knew everything Yabal had suffered. He Himself felt every insult, every rejection, every loss that Yabal had experienced. And His heart ached for him.

With a sob Yabal threw himself at Jesus' feet, pleading, "Lord, if You're willing, You can make me clean!"

Jesus dropped to His knees and wrapped His arms around him. His own tears wetting Yabal's rotting face, He whispered, "I will! Be clean!"

It all happened so fast Yabal felt for a moment that he must be dreaming. *Arms* around him! This couldn't be real. No one *touched* a leper! And no one had touched him in so many years he had almost forgotten what it felt like.

Suddenly he sensed a change in himself. He felt better—normal, healed! When he looked at his hands, they glowed with healthy skin. No scars, no scales, no rotting flesh. And he could *feel* them! He could feel his feet! In fact, he could feel his whole body. Cautiously he reached up to touch his nose. It was there! Now he could blink his eyes and see clearly.

But Jesus was talking to him, telling him that God loved him. His sickness was not a punishment. Satan makes bad things happen, but God makes people well.

"Now go show yourself to the priests," Jesus instructed. "And

don't tell anyone what happened."

But Yabal couldn't help telling everyone what happened. The priests pronounced him clean. And Yabal the leper became once again Yabal the husband, Yabal the father. And he never forgot Jesus, the Man who had touched him.

✕ ✕ ✕

By now, Stacey, Jason, and Marlene were desperate. They'd looked everywhere with no luck. Even Maria had gotten into the act, discreetly searching in every building and vacant lot clear to the edge of town.

The children spied the mayor practicing his speech behind city hall. They raced up to him and politely waited until he'd finished his presentation.

"And so, my friends and constituency," he said with a broad wave of his hand, "we must all stand behind this project with our financial support. This town needs a museum of antiquity. No, I say it *must have* this facility, not only for the education of our young people, but for the enjoyment and edification of generations to come. Folks will travel from bordering states, perhaps even from overseas, to view our fine collection of artifacts dating back thousands of years! Won't you join me in this brave new endeavor? I pledge my support to the community college, and I challenge you to do the same. Thank you."

Stacey and the others applauded loudly as the mayor bowed deeply at the waist. "That was a great speech," she called.

"Yeah," Jason added. "We'll probably raise a million dollars."

Mayor Deardorff grinned from ear to ear, his bald head shining in the bright afternoon sun. "Well, thank you, children," he said, adjusting his coat and straightening his bright-green tie. "Wrote it myself."

"I could tell," Marlene beamed, reaching out to shake the mayor's hand. "Made me want to empty my pockets right here and now in support of the museum."

The man smiled broadly. "Let's hope all the citizens of Valley Springs share our vision."

Stacey stepped forward. "Before you go, Mayor, have you

seen anything kinda out of the ordinary around here in the past hour?"

"Out of the ordinary?"

"Kinda weird," Stacey stated, twisting her face. "You know, peculiar looking, maybe a little scary?"

"Oh, you mean Deputy Steward's cousin Rosie?" The mayor rubbed his chin thoughtfully. "Last time I saw her was about four days ago at the post office. Poor woman. Maybe if she did something different with her hair . . ."

Stacey sighed. The joke was wearing thin. Was everyone a comedian? "You haven't seen anything stranger than that recently?"

The mayor shook his head. "I've *never* seen anything stranger than Cousin Rosie."

Glancing at his watch, the man suddenly stiffened. "Hey. Look at the time. I've gotta get to the staging area to meet with Dr. Morrison and Professor Appleby. I'll see you young people later. Gotta run!"

As he trotted away, he called over his shoulder, "If I see Rosie, I'll tell her you're looking for her."

Stacey sank to the pavement, a groan escaping her lips. "We're dead. They might as well come and say words over us, 'cause we're goners for sure."

Not too far away the crowd of youthful listeners surrounding the park bench had grown. Maggie B's cheery voice could just be heard above the excited din on the square.

✕ ✕ ✕

"Why do I have to take a lunch?" Nathan complained, eager to be on his way. "I'll be back in time to eat. I'm not going to stay all day, you know!"

Mother turned to face him. Her eyes held a familiar gleam that told him he had lost the battle. "Nathan, sit down and be still," she ordered.

"Now, you're going to take a lunch. From what I've heard, this Jesus is a wonderful storyteller. And if I know you—and I do—you'll be the last one to leave! You may even thank me for making you wait until I finish packing your lunch."

All the while Mother talked her hands had been busily wrapping five barley cakes and two small salted fish in pieces of cloth. Dropping the bundles into a basket, she handed it to Nathan. "Now run along," she said, giving him a quick hug. "Tell me all about Jesus when you get home!"

Nathan grinned in spite of himself. *I guess I'm glad I have a lunch to take with me,* he thought. With Mother's hug he suddenly felt happier.

"'Bye!" he shouted as he ran out the door and toward the lake.

At the water's edge he quickly untied a small boat, gave it a little shove, then leaped into it. In one smooth, practiced motion, he grabbed the oars and began to pull the boat out into the lake.

Nathan had learned to handle a boat almost as soon as he knew how to walk. Growing up as he had in a lakeside village, he felt as comfortable on the water as he did on land. Only recently, however, had his parents allowed him to take the boat out by himself.

So now, with the sun shining in his face and sparkling on the clear blue water, he felt quite grown-up. But most of all, he felt excited. Jesus had come back to Galilee after having been gone for a while. And this time he—Nathan—would get to see the story-telling, miracle-working Rabbi!

There certainly are a lot of boats on the lake this morning, Nathan thought to himself as he found himself surrounded by other vessels. Glancing around him, toward shore, he noticed crowds of people hiking along the water's edge. And they all headed in the same direction—toward the hill where Jesus had gone to be with His disciples.

Well, it is almost time for the Passover, Nathan continued thinking. *Lots of people pass this way as they journey toward Jerusalem. I guess they heard that Jesus is here, just as I did.*

At last the underside of his boat scraped the stony lake bottom, and he jumped out into the shallow water and pulled the boat up on shore. Instantly a mass of people engulfed him, and he found himself climbing with them up a grassy hillside.

Nathan had never seen so many people together in one place before. Men—fishermen and farmers, potters, matmakers, leather workers, blacksmiths, and carpenters—strained their eyes for a glimpse of Jesus. Young mothers scrambled up the slope, cradling babies in a kind of sling across their chests, while toddlers clung to their skirts. Grandmothers and grandfathers, leaning heavily on their walking sticks, shuffled their slow, determined way toward the top. And children of all ages climbed with strong young legs, their faces glowing.

Nathan's eyes danced with excitement. He was almost there, almost—almost—whew! With a final explosion of breath he reached the summit. And there, gazing right at him, stood a Man with a gentle air of authority. Nathan found himself unable to look away from the Man's warm eyes.

Suddenly the Man smiled. And that smile lit up His whole face.

Others crowded around Him, and Nathan felt himself being jostled and pushed as everyone tried to get close to the Man, this spellbinding Man who just had to be Jesus.

People swarmed over the grassy hilltop, thousands of them. Reaching out their hands to Jesus, many sought healing. And He disappointed no one. Nathan watched with open mouth as blind people sang out, "I can see!" He saw deaf people beam with wonder as the loving tones of Jesus fell on ears that could suddenly hear. People with all sorts of diseases came to Him and were healed.

And all the while Jesus spoke kind and gentle words. He described His Father in heaven. "He's your Father, too, you know," He assured them. "Don't be afraid to tell Him your troubles and to ask for things you need. He loves to give good gifts to His children."

Throughout the day He never sat down, never rested. He told the children stories, and Nathan listened with shining eyes.

Jesus' disciples noticed that their beloved Master had grown pale with weariness. "He needs to rest!" they whispered among themselves. "He tends to everyone else's needs but His own. He should send the people away."

Full of concern, they whispered in His ears, "Why don't You send the people away now? You must take some time for Yourself!"

But Jesus' only thought was for the needs of the people, who had left their homes and their work to come to see Him. So captivated were they by His words that they never noticed when mealtime came and went.

Of course, there was no place up here on the hillside to buy food. But Jesus had a wonderful idea of how to feed these people. He thought, however, that He would first ask His disciples for their ideas. Would they request Him to solve the problem, or would they depend on themselves in this emergency?

In the meantime Nathan's stomach had begun to growl. At first he paid no attention to the hollow feeling there. Then suddenly he remembered the basket he held in his hand.

A look of pure pleasure washed over his face as he lifted the cover and peeked inside. He stuck in one finger and pushed the cloth off his bread and fish. His mouth watered, and he wanted to eat, but somehow he didn't have the nerve, standing in the middle of a group of hungry people. He did not have enough to share with everybody.

Suddenly he strained his ears to hear what Jesus was saying. "Give the people something to eat," He instructed His disciples. Then, looking at Philip, He asked, "Where do you think we can buy bread?"

Philip stammered and stuttered as he gazed at the sea of people. "Why, we can't feed all these people! Why don't we just send them into town to buy bread for themselves? Besides, we don't have enough money to buy food for everyone. It would take eight months' wages!"

Jesus felt a pang of disappointment with Philip's answer. When would His disciples learn to trust Him for every need? But He answered Philip almost as if He hadn't heard his gloomy pronouncement. "How much food can we find in the crowd?" He asked.

Andrew, always in the habit of making himself useful, had already worked his way through the masses, noting anything unusual. And he had seen Nathan lift the corner of his little basket and peek inside.

"There's a boy here with five barley cakes and two small fish," he offered apologetically. "But what is that among so many?"

Jesus smiled. "Bring them to Me," He said.

With a look of complete bewilderment on his face, Andrew again found Nathan. "Uh, excuse me. Jesus asked if He might have your lunch."

Nathan's eyes opened wide. Jesus wanted his lunch? How wonderful! What an honor! Wait until Mother heard about this! "Sure!" he gulped, thrusting the basket into Andrew's hands. "He can have it!"

Still looking mystified, Andrew handed the basket to Jesus.

Jesus smiled as He looked over the waiting crowd. Then, turning to His disciples, He instructed, "Divide them up into groups of hundreds and fifties." And soon the grassy slope looked as if it were decorated with brightly colored flower beds as people with colorful clothing sat in orderly groups.

Andrew busily started counting. Five thousand men! And that wasn't even counting wives, mothers, grandmothers, children.

Still smiling, with the most joyous light in His eyes, Jesus invited people to join Him in thanking God for the food. And holding up Nathan's little lunch, He spoke to God. "Thank You, Father, for Your goodness in providing food for us. Blessed are those who eat it and the boy who shared it."

Nathan felt shivers run right up and down his spine. He knew that if he were any happier he would surely burst.

Then Jesus lifted up a barley cake and began to break it into smaller pieces. And He kept breaking it and breaking it and breaking it. Somehow that one little barley cake filled a whole big basket that someone found, and then the pieces of barley bread overflowed still another. Jesus broke the next barley cake, and the next, until all of them had managed to fill a batch of baskets with bread. Next He started to divide the fish. And more fish. And more fish.

Nathan stared. He rubbed his eyes. He shook his head. He must be dreaming. But no! His little lunch had grown, multiplied. And it increased even more as Jesus' disciples began passing it out to everyone.

Before long every person in that immense crowd had eaten their fill of Nathan's simple lunch. And when they had finished, Jesus sent the disciples to collect all the leftovers.

Leftovers! Nathan thought. This was just too much. His mind reeled with the wonder of it all. But the 12 disciples came back to Jesus, each carrying a full basket of food. *Twelve baskets of leftovers! Mother will never believe this!* Nathan thought.

With a warm smile Jesus said, "Give these baskets away to the poor."

Suddenly a great commotion swept the crowd. Someone had shouted, "He's a prophet just like Moses! He has fed us, just as Moses fed the Israelites in the wilderness with manna and quail!"

And another voice shouted, "Anoint Him king!" while still another set up the chant "Death to Rome! Death to Rome!"

Jesus' disciples joined the chant. In fact, they began to lead it. It was the opportunity they had waited for—the chance to make Jesus king! Now everyone would know that they were not following a false prophet or a raving rabbi.

"He's too modest to proclaim Himself king!" the excited disciples breathlessly explained to the reckless masses. "Let's grab Him and force Him to lead an army against Rome. Just think, with Him commanding the forces, the army would never go hungry! Come on, let's . . .!"

But Jesus had no desire to start a political revolution. He wanted to change people's hearts. Jesus had not performed a miracle to rally people around Him, but to satisfy their physical hunger when they were far from home and their spiritual hunger for the rest of their lives.

Jesus held up His hand, and the flash of authority in His eyes caused the crowd to fall silent. In firm but loving tones, He said to His disciples, "Go get in the boat, and head for Capernaum. I'll join you later."

But the disciples didn't want to leave. "This is the time!" they objected. And Judas argued, "If You disappoint these people today, they'll turn against You tomorrow!"

Jesus sighed. What Judas said was true. And He hadn't needed Judas to tell Him that. Still He insisted. "Go. Now." Reluctantly, slowly, the disciples made their way down the mountain.

Then, facing the crowd, He said, "Go home now." Feeling disappointed, but somehow unable to disobey that gentle command, they left.

Turning, Jesus walked into the hills. Far below Him He could see His disciples slowly trudging down the slope. Sinking to His knees, He began to pray. "Father, help My disciples to trust Me more. Help them to resist the temptation to doubt, and the desire for earthly greatness. Let Me fulfill Your will."

The sun blazed red and sank in the west. Peace returned to the hillside and spread across the lake in a fiery reflection of the sky. One by one, and in little groups, the people returned to their homes.

Nathan dipped the oars into the crimson water. His mind whirled with wonder—the wonder of Jesus.

A small smile suddenly lit his face. Mother had said he might thank her for that lunch! He pulled harder on the oars. Yes, he would. He certainly would.

⚔ ⚔ ⚔

"And that concludes our storytime for this afternoon," Mr. McDonald announced with excitement lifting his words. "I'm going to be off the air for the next couple hours in order to take part in the grand parade scheduled to begin in just five minutes. By the looks of the crowd outside my window, I doubt if any of my listeners are home anyway. So until later this evening, this is WPRL, Valley Springs, shutting down for a while. I'll be back after the parade."

The little radio on the park bench fell silent. An eager anticipation unlike the town had ever felt before filled the air.

The street surrounding the square was packed solid with smiling faces. Children laughed, dogs barked, and even the pigeons overhead seemed to cackle and chirp with renewed determination.

Stacey, Maria, Jason, and Marlene flopped down on the park bench, their faces uncharacteristically long and somber for such a happy occasion. For them the parade was turning into a disaster even before it began.

"I'm moving to Florida," Jason sighed. "They won't be able to find me there."

"Don't count on it," Maria chuckled.

Marlene shook her head. "Our parents will never speak to us again."

Stacey groaned. "Oh, mine will speak to me. Loud and clear. Just as soon as they let me out of the penitentiary."

Suddenly a piercing siren filled the air. The *thump, thump, thump* of a big bass drum immediately followed it. The parade was beginning right on schedule.

The children expected a roar of anticipation from the crowd, but what they heard instead was a collective gasp. Then everything was absolutely silent.

Stacey looked up and saw faces frozen in shock. Every eye was staring down the street in the direction from which the parade was supposed to come.

"What's going on?" Maria whispered.

The children elbowed their way to the front of the crowd. As they glanced to the right, their breath caught in their throats. "I don't believe it!" Jason declared, a smile lighting his face. "It's a miracle!"

There, standing straight and tall in front of the fire engine, looking to one side of the street, then to the other, was the biggest, ugliest, most amazing creature Valley Springs had ever seen.

"The camel!" Stacey shouted. *"There's our camel!"*

As if on cue, the animal began plodding down the avenue, head held high, eyes opened wide, wrinkled nose hovering over the biggest animal grin the children had ever seen.

A wild roar of approval echoed from the assembled throng as the dromedary, his tall hump swaying from side to side, thick hooves cloppity, cloppity, clopping over the pavement, ambled up the street toward the square. The sea of humanity fell back, leaving a wide passageway for the creature.

Jason shook his head in disbelief. "He doesn't even need us to guide him. That critter's doin' just fine by himself. Hey, Marlene, there's your royal steed. Go get on board."

"Oh, sure," the girl chuckled. "You think I'm going to run out there and shimmy up those hairy legs and swaying hump in front of all these people? No, I'll just watch the parade from here if you don't mind."

The men driving the fire truck, encouraged by their hairy leader, revved their engine, sounded their horn, wound up their siren, switched on every light the vehicle had, and moved majestically along behind the animal.

The high school band blasted the air with a dozen trumpets and surged forward as one, their stomping feet marching in time to their music.

Stacey, Maria, Jason, and Marlene watched openmouthed as the subject of their desperate search strutted by, oblivious to the hour of agony he had brought with his wandering ways.

But the children didn't care anymore. He was leading the parade, just as he was supposed to, just as he'd been trained to by his skillful handlers at the circus.

Stacey cheered and cheered, her voice mingling with the energetic shouts of the townspeople. When the car carrying Mayor Deardorff, Dr. Morrison, and Professor Appleby passed slowly by, the girl knew all the hard work had been worth it. The populace of Valley Springs provided an almost deafening welcome to their favorite citizens.

A happy tear crept down Stacey's cheek. Professor Appleby looked so proud, all dressed up in his favorite red sweater, blue trousers, yellow shirt, and purple bow tie. For too long he'd been the subject of whispered ridicule and unfounded gossip. Now his loving personality and genuine regard for others would be fully revealed in a most spectacular way. Stacey knew her grandfather's life was about to change forever, thanks to his undying love for Maggie B and the cause she lived for.

Without thinking, the girl reached over and gave Marlene a big hug. Her companion grinned. "Not bad for a bunch of kids and one crazy old man," she asserted.

Stacey nodded. "Like Jason said, it's a miracle."

The girl felt someone tap her firmly on the shoulder as a deep, raspy voice called over the cheering throng. "You, Stacey Roth? I'm Rosie. Mayor Deardorff said you were lookin' for me."

The color drained from Stacey's face. Out on the street the parade continued, led by the surprise mascot with the really stupendous, amazing, absolutely extraordinary smile.

BIBLE PLACES

```
Z  N  I  P  M  M  E  T  R  N  I  L  E  K  F
C  U  U  J  E  E  U  D  X  A  E  L  U  A  P
L  B  X  N  N  L  K  X  H  G  P  S  M  A  J
C  I  R  B  U  A  R  C  Y  F  E  R  L  R  O
G  A  E  O  H  S  C  P  Y  M  N  E  A  N  I
W  H  P  G  S  U  T  A  O  X  S  P  A  H  O
G  T  H  E  S  R  S  R  P  T  X  D  D  Y  P
S  I  I  N  M  E  X  D  I  E  R  B  V  X  G
U  R  D  N  J  J  D  N  K  O  R  Y  R  F  J
C  E  I  E  M  H  E  G  J  E  U  N  O  O  Z
S  H  M  S  X  T  Z  A  R  E  P  H  A  T  H
A  C  C  A  T  Q  M  W  A  B  A  N  A  U  V
M  P  A  R  O  S  Y  R  I  A  I  I  O  G  M
A  T  N  E  S  I  L  S  H  A  D  U  J  C  H
D  J  A  T  O  F  N  A  A  N  A  C  W  I  X
```

Abana	Jerusalem	Rome
Cana	Jordan	Shunem
Canaan	Judah	Syria
Capernaum	Nile	Zarephath
Cherith	Nubia	
Damascus	Palestine	
Egypt	Pharpar	
Gennesaret	Rephidim	

Is There a Healer in the House?

L ife in biblical times was extremely hard. People died early. Most children perished in infancy or childhood. According to tombstones and other inscriptions dating from New Testament times, the most common ages of death for those who reached adulthood were 27 for women and 29 for men. Accident, war, and famine killed many, but disease threatened everyone.

Diet was limited and poor, and crowding and poor sanitation made the villages and towns hotbeds for disease. When an army attacked a city, it was a race between capturing the city or the army itself perishing from some sickness the soldiers would spread as they crowded together in their camps outside the city walls. People working in certain types of jobs had their own unique illnesses. Stone cutters, for example, suffered from lung diseases caused by breathing rock dust. Studies of the bones found in graves dramatically show the effects of bad diet, working too hard, and dampness and other harsh living conditions.

The Old Testament has a number of laws and regulations about disease, but they mostly involve quarantine—the prevention of a disease's spread by isolating those who already have it. The ancient world knew little about the physical cause of illness. They regarded disease as supernatural punishment for breaking divine law. Even God's people considered illness as punishment for sin. Thus a deadly fever was not the result of microbes entering the body but a divine penalty for having done something wrong. The people of the Bible would have considered Job's boils or the blindness of the man whose sight Jesus restored to be the result of something wrong either the victims or their family had done.

The ancient world made little scientific study of disease. Even the way they described diseases shows this. They lumped various illnesses together by common, superficial traits. For example, the Israelites grouped all kinds of skin diseases under the term *leprosy.*

According to the book of Leviticus, the walls of a house or fabric material could have leprosy (Lev. 13:49; 14:37), suggesting that here appearance was their prime category for labeling the disease, not its cause or physiological symptom. The mold attacking a mud-plastered wall or a damp linen garment created markings similar to those of skin diseases, so the ancients assumed they must all be the same thing.

Because they considered that touching a dead body made a person ritually unclean, the Jews did not dissect and study the body. They had little knowledge of anatomy and physiology. What they did know they probably learned from the Egyptians, who had picked it up while embalming mummies.

Ancient physicians did have some surgical skills, however. Archaeologists in the Holy Land occasionally unearth sets of surgical instruments that are in many ways similar to those used today. Doctors such as the Gentile Gospel writer Luke could set broken bones, lance boils, and bind up wounds, but they had few medicines except for herbs and similar natural substances. If people did not recover from disease through the body's natural healing processes, herbal remedies, or bathing in hot mineral springs, they then turned to prayer, magic, and the help of those who seemed to be endowed with supernatural power to heal. Few had the money to hire expensive physicians with even their limited medical skills and knowledge.

Jesus' power to heal brought great hope to a world that lived in constant fear of disease and illness. And He did not consider illness to be a punishment for sin, but the natural danger of living in an imperfect world.

ANSWERS TO PUZZLES

BEFORE AND AFTER

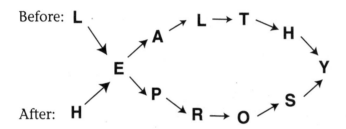

GOD'S LOVE REBUS

Answers:
ARM + SNAKE + TRAIN - STAR - KITE - R = MANNA
QUEEN + PAIL + NEST - PEN - NET - E = QUAIL
FAWN + CAT + BEAR - FAN - CAB = WATER

FIND BABY MOSES

ELIJAH FED BY RAVENS

Answer: God Cares

BIBLE PEOPLE

```
J  P  I  L  I  H  P  H  B  E  C  O  O  F  J
J  M  B  H  M  L  A  N  L  O  H  J  Z  C  S
E  A  D  U  X  U  K  I  H  A  E  Y  K  C  H
Y  I  Q  L  P  E  J  A  I  H  G  J  T  G  A
E  R  C  D  V  A  I  L  O  G  A  Y  B  U  R
M  I  J  J  A  H  S  A  S  O  H  K  W  U  V  H
A  M  V  H  O  H  H  U  A  J  E  S  U  S  P
R  A  N  J  T  E  J  B  H  R  J  W  R  B  I
M  A  A  A  B  N  J  O  D  E  J  U  Y  K  H
A  R  M  A  V  H  F  N  C  E  J  J  B  O  S
R  O  A  T  U  Z  A  Q  Z  H  L  Y  B  U  E
E  N  A  R  M  O  S  E  S  L  E  I  H  E  G
K  E  N  F  X  B  B  S  C  I  M  B  S  H  I
R  O  L  X  C  E  J  X  C  X  T  K  E  H  X
O  B  J  Y  L  D  W  J  R  V  Y  J  O  D  A
```

BIBLE PLACES

```
Z  N  I  P  M  M  E  T  R  N  I  L  E  K  F
C  U  U  J  E  E  U  D  X  A  E  L  U  A  P
L  B  X  N  L  K  X  H  G  P  S  M  A  J
C  I  R  B  U  A  R  C  Y  F  E  R  L  R  O
G  A  E  O  H  S  C  P  Y  M  N  E  A  N  I
W  H  P  G  S  U  T  A  O  X  S  P  A  H  O
G  T  H  E  S  R  S  R  P  T  X  D  Y  P
S  I  I  N  M  E  X  D  I  E  R  B  V  X  G
U  R  D  N  J  J  D  N  K  O  R  Y  R  F  J
C  E  I  E  M  H  E  G  J  E  U  N  O  O  Z
S  H  M  S  X  T  Z  A  R  E  P  H  A  T  H
A  C  C  A  T  Q  M  W  A  B  A  N  A  U  V
M  P  A  R  O  S  Y  R  I  A  I  I  O  G  M
A  T  N  E  S  I  L  S  H  A  D  U  J  C  H
D  J  A  T  O  F  N  A  A  N  A  C  W  I  X
```

The Shadow Creek Ranch Series
by Charles Mills

1. Escape to Shadow Creek Ranch
Joey races through New York City's streets with a deadly secret in his pocket. It's the start of an escape that introduces him to a loving God, a big new family, and life on a Montana ranch.

2. Mystery in the Attic
Something's hidden in the attic. Wendy insists it's a curse. Join her as she faces a seemingly life-threatening mystery that ultimately reveals a wonderful secret about God's power.

3. Secret of Squaw Rock
A group of young guests comes to the ranch, each with a past to escape and a future to discover. Share in the exciting events that bring changes to their troubled lives.

4. Treasure of the Merrilee
Wendy won't talk about what she found in the mountains, and Joey's nowhere to be found! Book 4 takes you into the hearts of two of your favorite characters as you see events change their lives forever.

5. Whispers in the Wind
Through the eyes of your friends at the ranch, experience the worst storm in Montana's history and a Power stronger than the fiercest winds, more lasting than the darkest night.

6. Heart of the Warrior

The deadly object arrives without warning. Suddenly Joey realizes he's about to face the greatest challenge of his young life. He's answered threats like this before. But never from an Indian.

7. River of Fear

A horse expedition brings Joey and Wendy face-to-face with the terrifying results of sin. Wendy goes for help, but soon finds herself in more trouble than anyone else.

8. Danger in the Depths

Wendy Hanson is missing. Her father and friends from Shadow Creek Ranch frantically begin to search. But every clue draws them closer to the unthinkable!

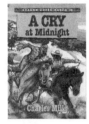

9. A Cry at Midnight

It's winter camp at Shadow Creek Ranch, and one camper's heart is frozen in pain. Exciting adventures help her discover a loving God who longs to heal.

10. Attack of the Angry Legend

It's more than 10 feet tall, weighs almost a ton, and is headed straight for the station! Your friends at Shadow Creek Ranch are about to meet one of nature's most ferocious creatures.

Paperbacks, US$5.99, Cdn$8.49 each.
